Charles Dickens's
A TALE OF
TWO CITIES

D0366512

Henry I. Hubert
Department of English
University of Kentucky

Revised and Edited by
Stephanie Muntone

1997 Barnes & Noble Books

MACMILLAN is a registered trademark of Macmillan, Inc.
Monarch and colophons are trademarks of Simon & Schuster, Inc.,
registered in the U.S. Patent and Trademark Office.

Macmillan Publishing USA
A division of Simon & Schuster, Inc.
1633 Broadway
New York, NY 10019

ISBN 0-7607-0834-7

Text design by Tony Meisel

Printed and bound in the United States of America.

99 00 01 M 9 8 7 6

RRDC

CONTENTS

INTRODUCTION TO CHARLES DICKENS

EARLY LIFE

Charles Dickens was born on February 7, 1812, in Portsea, England. His father, John Dickens, was a minor clerk in the Naval Pay Office; his father's parents had been servants and his mother's parents only slightly higher on the social scale. John Dickens was a happy-go-lucky, improvident man whose family often knew want as the debts piled up. At the age of twelve, Charles Dickens experienced what was to become the key event of his life. John Dickens was imprisoned for debt in London's Marshalsea Prison; young Charles was taken out of school and put to work in a blacking warehouse in London, pasting labels on bottles of shoe polish. Although he later returned to school for a time, this experience left a permanent mark on his soul. Even many years later, after he had become a successful author, he could not bear to talk about it, or be reminded of his family's ignominy.

At the age of fifteen, Dickens began working as an office boy for a law firm. He taught himself shorthand, and by 1828 he became a reporter for the lay courts of Doctors' Common. The dull routine of the legal profession never interested him, so he became a newspaper reporter for the *Mirror of Parliament*, *The True Sun*, and finally for the *Morning Chronicle*. (John Forster, later his closest friend and biographer, was also employed at *The True Sun*.) By the age of twenty, Dickens was one of the best Parliamentary reporters in all of England.

During this same period Dickens' interest began to switch from journalism to literature. His first work of fiction, "Dinner at Poplar Walk" (later reprinted as "Mr. Minns and His Cousin"), appeared in the *Monthly Magazine* when he was twenty-one. His newspaper work had given him an intimate knowledge of the streets and byways of London, and late in 1832 he began writing sketches and stories of London life. They began to appear in periodicals and newspapers in 1833, and in 1836 they were gathered together as *Sketches by Boz, Illustrations of Every-day Life*, and *Every-day People*. This pseudonym, Boz, was suggested by his brother's pronunciation of "Moses" when he had a cold.

THE PICKWICK PAPERS

The success of the *Sketches* brought an invitation from the publishers Chapman and Hall in 1836 to furnish the "letterpress," or captions, for a series of cartoon sketches about a humorous cockney sporting club. The project had hardly begun when Robert Seymour, the artist, committed suicide. Dickens searched for a new artist and found an ideal collaborator in H. K. Browne ("Phiz"), but in the meantime Dickens persuaded the publisher to let him improvise a fictional narrative. When the *Posthumous Papers of the Pickwick Club* finally came out, the story predominated over the illustrations.

When the *Pickwick Papers* appeared in April 1836, as a monthly serial, the sales were discouraging. Of the first issue, a modest 400 copies were printed; later the work became increasingly popular. Some 40,000 copies of each issue were sold. After the last installment appeared in November 1837, the novel was published in book form. This set the pattern for all of Dickens' subsequent novels.

The success of *Pickwick* convinced Dickens that his real career lay in writing fiction; he gave up his Parliamentary reporting in order to devote himself to it full time. In 1836 he had married Catherine Hogarth, the daughter of one of the owners of the *Morning Chronicle*; his growing family made it necessary to work exhaustingly at his writing. His next work, *Oliver Twist*, began appearing even before *Pickwick* was completed. *Nicholas Nickleby* followed in a like manner in 1838–39, and the very first number sold some 50,000 copies. Dickens was horrified over the conditions in rural boys' schools in England and the helplessness of the children. Both *Oliver*

Twist and *Nicholas Nickleby* exposed these conditions to the public eye; Dickens became a powerful voice for social reform. During this same period he was editor of *Bentley's Miscellany* (1837–39). By the 1840s Dickens had become the most popular novelist in Britain, taking over the place long held by Sir Walter Scott.

THE MIDDLE YEARS

The years between 1840 and 1855 were most fruitful ones: *The Old Curiosity Shop, Barnaby Rudge, A Christmas Carol, Martin Chuzzlewit, Dombey and Son, David Copperfield, Bleak House, Little Dorrit,* and *Hard Times* all appeared. In addition, he made his first trip to America; copyright laws at that time allowed American publishers to pirate his works, and their lack of concern over this injustice undoubtedly contributed to Dickens' unfavorable criticism of America in *Martin Chuzzlewit*. In 1850 Dickens founded his own periodical, Household Words, and continued to edit it until he and his partner exchanged it for *All the Year Round* in 1859. *Hard Times, A Tale of Two Cities,* and *Great Expectations* appeared in serial form in these publications. But these years of literary success were marred by domestic strife. Dickens and Catherine Hogarth had never been particularly suited to each other, and their marriage ended in separation in 1856.

In addition to writing, Dickens had another love—amateur theatricals—which led him into yet another pursuit in the latter part of his career. He gave public readings from his novels from 1859 to 1868 in England, Scotland, and America. He had always loved the theater—he studied drama as a young man and had organized an amateur theatrical company of his own in 1847 (he was both manager and principal actor).

THE LATTER YEARS

His energies never seemed to fail: He burned the candle at both ends. He published *Our Mutual Friend* in 1864–65 and at his death left an unfinished novel, *The Mystery of Edwin*

Drood, a tale of suspense. He died suddenly in 1870 from a stroke. G. K. Chesterton once said that Dickens died of "popularity." It would seem so; his exhaustive burden (marked by insomnia and fatigue) is well catalogued in his letters. He was buried in the Poets' Corner of Westminster Abbey.

Dickens wrote with an eye on the tastes of a wide readership, never far ahead of the printer, and he was always ready to modify a story to suit his readers. For example, when the sales of serial installments of *Martin Chuzzlewit* fell from 60,000 to 20,000, Dickens sent his hero off to America in order to stimulate renewed interest. No novelist ever had so close a relationship with his public, a public ranging from barely literate factory girls to wealthy dowagers, but consisting mostly of the newly formed middle classes.

TEACHER AND ENTERTAINER

In *The English Novel*, Walter Allen points out that Dickens became the spokesman for this rising middle class, and was also its teacher. "Dickens more than any of his contemporaries was the expression of the conscience—untutored, baffled, muddled as it doubtless often was—of his age," he writes. Not only in his novels, but in his magazine, *Household Words*, Dickens lashed out at what he considered the worst social abuses of his time: imprisonment for debt, the ferocious penal code, the unsanitary slums that bred criminals, child labor, the widespread mistreatment of children, the unsafe machinery in factories, and the hideous schools.

Yet, as Allen suggests, Dickens was primarily a great entertainer, "the greatest entertainer, probably, in the history of fiction." It is significant that Dickens was not satisfied to have his books the best sellers of their time. He wanted to see his audience, to manipulate it with the power of his own words. His public readings gave him an excellent opportunity to do so. Sitting alone on a bare stage, he would read excerpts from various novels, act them out really, imitating the voices of the various characters. These theatrical readings would always contain at least one sentimental scene, which would move the audience to tears. Dickens suffered all the emotions with his audience, even after repeated readings, and this undoubtedly helped to shorten his life. He entertained his readers with humor, pathos, suspense, and melodrama, all on a grand scale. Charles Dickens had a fertile imagination that peopled his novels with characters and events that continue to entertain twentieth-century readers as they delighted his contemporaries.

NOVEL TECHNIQUE

An understanding of Dickens as an artist requires an understanding of the method of publication he used—monthly or weekly installments. Serialization left its mark on his fiction and often accounts for the flaws that many critics have found in his work. John Butt and Kathleen Tillotson in *Dickens at Work* (1957) describe the problems serial publication imposed:

Chapters must be balanced within a number in respect both of length and of effect. Each number must lead, if not to a climax, at least to a point of rest; and the rest between numbers is necessarily more extended than what the mere chapter divisions provide. The writer had also to bear in mind that his readers were constantly interrupted for prolonged periods, and that he must take this into account in his characterizations and, to some extent, in his plotting.

This technique brought on a loose, episodic treatment with a vast, intricate plot, numerous characters, and much repetition to jog the reader's memory. Instead of the whole novel slowly building to a real climax, each part had to have a little climax of its own. In *Hard Times* the bad effects of serialization are at a minimum because it is a comparatively short novel (about 260 pages in most editions) and it appeared in weekly rather than monthly parts. But the careful reader can still tell where each part ended; considerations of space rather than of artistic technique formed the story.

The works of Dickens have many of their roots in the eighteenth century, especially in the novels of Tobias Smollett, whom he greatly admired. From Smollett he borrowed many devices of characterization, tagging characters with physical peculiarities, speech mannerisms, compulsive gestures, and eccentric names. Examples in *Hard Times* include the distinctive speech pattern of Stephen Blackpool, who talks in a phonetically transcribed Lancashire dialect; the self-deprecating speech of Bounderby or the self-pitying talk of Mrs. Sparsit; the physical peculiarities of Bitzer, the epitome of pallidness; the names of characters—Bounderby, M'Choakumchild, Gradgrind—so evocative of their personalities. The eighteenth-century theater, with its sharply defined villains, its involved melodramatic plots, and its farcical humor, also suggested ideas for plots and characterizations to Dickens.

Dickens took his descriptive techniques from Sir Walter Scott and other early nineteenth-century novelists. No character, no matter how minor, appears on the scene without being fully described, not only as to physical appearance, but also as to the clothing he wears. Dickens also excels in the short but evocative description of places; in *Hard Times* note the portrayal of the murky streets and factories of Coketown and of its blighted wasteland-like countryside.

THE WORLD OF HIS NOVELS

The world of Dickens' novels is a fantasy world, a fairy-tale world, a nightmare world. It is a world seen as through the eyes of a child: The shadows are blacker, the fog denser, the houses higher, the midnight streets emptier and more terrifying than in reality. To a child, inanimate objects have lives of their own: Thus the smoke malevolently winds over Coketown like serpents and the pistons of the steam engines in the factory are "melancholy mad elephants."

The characters, too, are seen as children see people. Their peculiarities are heightened to eccentricities; their vices, to monstrous proportions. Most of the people in his novels are caricatures, characterized by their externals, almost totally predictable in behavior. We know little about them beyond their surface behavior; Dickens focuses on the outward man, not the inner motives. It is interesting to note, however, that Dickens was able to create intensely individual portraits even though he lacked the ability to analyze motivation and character developments. His characters are more than types or mere abstract representations of virtue or vice. They are intensely alive and thus memorable. The characters from a Dickens novel are remembered long after the plots and even the titles of the books have been forgotten.

DICKENS THE REFORMER

Dickens in his lifetime saw Great Britain change from a rural, agricultural country of inns, stagecoaches, and fox-hunting squires to an urbanized, commercial-industrial land of railroads, factories, and slums. These changes are chronicled in his novels, and it is possible to read them as a social history of England. *Pickwick*, although set in 1827–28, reflects much of what still survived of the old eighteenth-century way of life. *Oliver Twist* (1837–39) shows the first impact of the Industrial Revolution—the poverty existing at that time and the feeble attempt to remedy it by workhouses. *Dombey and Son* (1846–48) describes the coming of the railroad, a symbol of change. Dombey, the merchant, sacrifices love, wife, and children for a position of power through money; yet he is already obsolete, for the industrialist is the ruler now.

Dickens grew increasingly bitter with each novel; his criticism of society became more radical, his satire more biting and less sweetened by humor. In his later novels he often broke out in indignant exasperation and almost hysterical anger. He figuratively mounted a soapbox, demanding that the "Lords and Gentlemen" do something about the appalling conditions of the poor.

In his early novels, society itself is not evil; it is only some people who are bad and who create misery for others by their callousness and neglect. By the time of *Dombey and Son* it is institutions that are evil, representing in that novel the self-expanding power of accumulated money. *Bleak House* (1852–53) attacks the law's delay and the self-perpetuating mass of futility it has become. *Hard Times* (1854) savagely lampoons the economic theories that Dickens considered responsible for much of human misery. The English historian Lord Macaulay charged that it was full of "sullen Socialism." Of *Little Dorrit* (1855–57), which attacks prisons and imprisonment for debt, George Bernard Shaw said that it was "more seditious than Karl Marx." In *Our Mutual Friend* (1864–65) we see the fully disillusioned Dickens. The atmosphere of the novel is grim, permeated with a sense of growing nightmare. There is the feeling that something deep and basic is wrong with the social order, something beyond the mere reforming of bad people or poorly run institutions.

BRIEF SUMMARY

BOOK ONE

It is 1775. Mr. Jarvis Lorry, a representative of Tellson's Bank in London, is sent to Paris to meet a newly released prisoner of the Bastille, Doctor Alexandre Manette, in Paris, to reunite him with his grown daughter Lucie, and to bring them both back to London. Born shortly after her father was thrown into prison eighteen years earlier, Lucie has grown up believing that she is an orphan. Mr. Lorry meets her at Dover, breaks the news to her, and escorts her to Paris.

Ernest Defarge, keeper of a wine-shop in the Saint Antoine neighborhood of Paris and a former servant of Dr. Manette, has looked after the doctor since his release from prison. Defarge takes Lorry and Lucie to a garret room where they see an old, white-haired man making shoes: It is Doctor Manette, who took up the trade in prison and who now thinks of himself only as an imprisoned shoemaker. His eighteen years of solitary confinement have nearly destroyed his memory and sanity. Arrangements are made for Lorry and the Manettes to leave for London immediately.

BOOK TWO

It is 1780. One day, Jerry Cruncher, a messenger for Tellson's Bank, is told to go to the Old Bailey, London's Criminal Courts Building, to await a message from Mr. Lorry, who is there. Jerry proceeds to the Old Bailey and finds a sensational trial in progress. Charles Darnay is accused of treason; specifically, of being a French spy. Several witnesses appear, including Mr. Lorry, Dr. Manette, and Lucie, all of whom met Darnay on the packet boat sailing from Calais to Dover on that night five years ago when Dr. Manette was brought to London. Things look dark for Darnay, but Mr. Stryver, Darnay's counsel, manages to blacken the characters of two of the witnesses, and Stryver's assistant, Sydney Carton, upsets the positive identification of a third by calling attention to a striking resemblance between himself and the prisoner Darnay. Darnay is acquitted. While Darnay is being congratulated after the trial, a look of fear and doubt crosses Dr. Manette's face, as if an old memory was awakened by Darnay.

At this time in France, the clouds of the coming revolution darken the skies as the downtrodden peasants work and starve to fatten the coffers of the nobility. One nobleman, a Marquis, on his way home from a lavish ball, crushes a child beneath the wheels of his coach and is quite unconcerned about it, tossing a gold coin to the stricken father. That evening, the Marquis receives a visitor at his chateau: his nephew, Charles Darnay, who has come once again to attempt to persuade his uncle to improve the lot of the peasantry, but with no success. Later in the evening, the Marquis is slain in his bed and the clouds of revolution grow blacker in the night sky.

In the five years that have passed since the end of Book One, Dr. Manette has been restored to his old self through Lucie's tender care and father and daughter live in a modest lodging, with Miss Pross, Lucie's old nurse, as maid and general housekeeper. Dr. Manette has recovered so completely that he is practicing medicine again. Both Charles Darnay and Sydney Carton have fallen in love with Lucie Manette on the occasion of her appearance at Darnay's trial. Carton, who is a slovenly, debauched man, knows that it would be fruitless to woo Lucie, but he visits her and pledges her his eternal friendship and devotion. Darnay approaches Dr. Manette to reveal his love for Lucie. Dr. Manette is visibly disturbed by this news of Darnay's affection for his daughter, but promises to give his blessing to a marriage if Lucie should express her love for Darnay.

A new royal spy is commissioned for the Saint Antoine quarter of Paris. It is John Barsad, who was one of the witnesses at Darnay's trial. The word travels rapidly to the wine-shop and to the ears of Monsieur and Madame Defarge, leaders of the underground conspiracy that will soon give the signal for revolution. Barsad arrives at the wine-shop to try to get some information concerning the unrest of the peasantry, but the Defarges give nothing away. Only when he reveals the news that Lucie is to wed Charles Darnay, nephew of the murdered Marquis, does Defarge show any emotion. The spy makes a mental note of this and leaves.

Lucie's wedding day arrives and, as had been agreed beforehand, Darnay reveals his true identity to Dr. Manette before the ceremony. Lucie and Charles are married and they leave on their honeymoon. Darnay's revelation has a traumatic effect on Dr. Manette; he loses his stability and once again thinks he is a shoemaker in a Bastille cell. After nine days, however, he recovers with no seeming ill effects, and as he goes off to join Lucie and Charles, Mr. Lorry and Miss Pross destroy his shoemaking equipment. Sydney Carton arrives at the house shortly after the Darnays' return and asks Darnay if they can be friends, to which request Darnay assents heartily.

Meanwhile, the situation in France has worsened and many nobles are fleeing France for their lives, taking whatever valuables they can with them or having them sent to England. Mr. Lorry is kept busy at the bank, for Tellson's has a French office and does much business with its French customers. Mr. Lorry is asked by the bank to return to Paris once more to try to straighten out the bank's affairs there, which are in chaos. On the day of his departure, he and Charles Darnay are conversing at Tellson's when a letter is brought. It is addressed to the Marquis Saint Evrémonde, Charles' true name, which has been concealed from everyone except Dr. Manette. Darnay takes the letter and promises to deliver it. Later, he reads it and learns that it is from a representative of his in France who has been arrested by the new revolutionary government, and whose life is threatened for being a representative of a hated nobleman. Darnay resolves to return to Paris to save the man's life.

BOOK THREE

Darnay leaves London that night and finally reaches Paris. Upon his arrival in Paris, he is thrown into prison. Dr. Manette and Lucie, along with Miss Pross and little Lucie, rush to Paris when they hear of Charles' fate. Dr. Manette, as a former prisoner in the Bastille, has great influence with the revolutionary government and he manages to keep Charles safe though he is unable to arrange his release. The other prisoners, meanwhile, are being slaughtered in droves.

Finally, many months later, Darnay is brought to trial and, through Dr. Manette's influence, is released. Darnay returns to Lucie's loving arms, but within twenty-four hours he is arrested again: this time accused by the Defarges and one other person. At the trial, the one other person turns out to be Dr. Manette himself, and the cause of Darnay's arrest is an old diary the doctor wrote while he was in prison and that was found by Defarge on the day the Bastille fell. In this diary Dr. Manette cursed the Evrémonde family for causing his imprisonment, and Charles Darnay, a member of the family, is thus cursed by the doctor as well. Darnay is sentenced to die within twenty-four hours.

Dr. Manette attempts once again to have him released, but to no avail. But Sydney Carton, who has arrived in Paris, conceives a scheme to spare Darnay's life. He forces John Barsad, who is now a spy for the prisons, to aid him in the scheme. He manages to visit Darnay's cell, change clothes with the prisoner, drug him, and have him taken out by Barsad to a coach, where Mr. Lorry is waiting with Lucie and Dr. Manette. Carton remains in the cell in Darnay's place and is executed the following day.

Madame Defarge, meanwhile, in her hatred for the Saint Evrémonde family, decides that the whole family must be wiped out and, accordingly, she proceeds to Lucie's lodgings. However, only Miss Pross is there, and in a struggle between the two women, Madame Defarge is killed, while the people who were the objects of her hatred flee to England and safety.

CHARACTERS

Jarvis Lorry, a representative of Tellson's Bank and friend of the Manettes

Jerry Cruncher, a messenger and odd-job man at Tellson's Bank

Lucie Manette, daughter of Dr. Manette, afterwards married to Charles Darnay

Miss Pross, servant of Lucie Manette

Ernest Defarge, keeper of a wine-shop in Paris, husband of Madame Defarge, also Jacques Four

Gaspard, a citizen of Paris

Madame (Therese) Defarge, keeper of a wine-shop in Paris, wife of Ernest Defarge

Jacques One, Jacques Two, and ***Jacques Three,*** revolutionists

Dr. Alexandre Manette, former prisoner of the Bastille, a physician

Mrs. Cruncher, wife of Jerry Cruncher

Young Jerry Cruncher, their son

Mr. Stryver, a barrister

Sydney Carton, a barrister, assistant to Mr. Stryver

Charles Saint Evrémonde, known as ***Charles Darnay***, an emigrant French aristocrat, later married to Lucie Manette

Little Lucie, Charles and Lucie's daughter

John Barsad, a spy and informer, first in London, later in Paris

Roger Cly, an Old Bailey spy, friend of John Barsad

Marquis Saint Evrémonde, a French nobleman, uncle of Charles Darnay

A Mender of Roads, later Jacques Five

Theophile Gabelle, a postmaster and bailiff of the Saint Evrémonde estate

The Vengeance, Madame Defarge's closest friend and ally

DETAILED ANALYSIS
BOOK THE FIRST: RECALLED TO LIFE

CHAPTER 1: THE PERIOD

This brief introductory chapter sets the time and place of the action: England and France, in 1775. Dickens observes the exaggerated praise and criticism of the age, noting that it is the same at present (1859); one still hears extravagant praise and extravagant blame of the times. He describes the French and English monarchs and mentions several news items of the year, including the American Revolution. He emphasizes that in both France and England, it is an age of violence: religious persecution in France, crime in England. He also comments that trees were already growing in 1775 that "the Woodsman, Fate," had already appointed to be cut down and made into boards for "a certain moveable framework," and that "the Farmer, Death," had already set aside certain rough oxcarts to be the tumbrils of the French Revolution.

COMMENT

Dickens' opening, in which he contrasts the praise and blame of the people of the age, is one of his most famous sentences. It runs the full paragraph and is an excellent example of parallel structure, which involves repetition of grammatical structures with varying phrases. "It was the best of times, it was the worst of times, it was the age of wisdom, it was the age of foolishness. . . ." Both the length of the sentences and the extensive use of parallel structure are hallmarks of Dickens' style.

Dickens makes a number of allusions to real people and events of 1775. The king and queen of England at the time were George III and Charlotte; the king and queen of France were Louis XVI and Marie Antoinette. The young Frenchman who was executed for not kneeling to a passing procession of monks was the Chevalier de la Barre, who was tortured and executed in the town of Abbeville in July 1766.

CHAPTER 2: THE MAIL

The coach that delivers the mail between London and Dover is laboring up Shooter's Hill through the mud with its contents. Beside it, to ease the strain on the horses, walk its three passengers while the coachman and a guard sit atop the coach. Frequent robberies of the mail by highwaymen account for the presence of the guard and also for the reserve of the three passengers, each of whom keeps to himself.

As the coach reaches the summit of the hill and pauses for the passengers to reclaim their seats, a horseman is heard approaching. Fear overcomes the passengers as the guard shouts out to the unseen horseman to halt. After stating his business, the horseman is permitted to approach while the guard stands warily with his gun at the ready. The rider is Jerry Cruncher, a messenger from the venerable London bank of Tellson's with a message for Mr. Jarvis Lorry, a representative of the bank who is a passenger in the coach and who is bound for Paris. The message reads "Wait at Dover for Mam'selle." In reply, Mr. Lorry gives Jerry the message, "Recalled to life." The coach rumbles on its way again while the coachman and guard puzzle over the reply. As the sounds of the coach fade in the distance, Jerry, left in the road, also considers Mr. Lorry's reply, but can make no sense of it. He decides that he, Jerry, would be in a "blazing bad way if recalling to life was to come into fashion."

COMMENT

This chapter sets the tone for the novel. It takes place at night, in an atmosphere of danger and suspicion. It includes the element of travel between London and Paris. Proving one's identity is crucial to one's safety in the chapter. It includes elements of mystery, not identifying all the characters or the errands on which they are bound. It contains the first of many references to "recalling to life," or resurrection.

The chapter introduces two of the novel's main characters, Jarvis Lorry and Jerry Cruncher. The plot begins to develop as Dickens presents the reader with two mysteries: What is Mr. Lorry's business in France, and who is the "Mam'selle" for whom he is to wait at Dover? Dickens also allows the reader to wonder about Jerry's reference to the harm it would do him if recalling to life were to "come into fashion."

CHAPTER 3: THE NIGHT SHADOWS

As Jerry Cruncher rides back to London, mulling over the message he is to deliver to Tellson's Bank, Mr. Lorry continues on his way to Dover. He whiles away the journey thinking over business matters, but finds his thoughts returning to the purpose of his present errand: He is on his way to dig someone out of a grave. In his mind, he sees a multitude of faces, all worn and wasted, the hair prematurely white; and to Mr. Lorry's unspoken question, "Buried how long?" the answer comes, "Almost eighteen years." "I hope you care to live?" "I can't say." He asks this ghost whether he cares "to see her," and here Mr. Lorry cannot predict the answer.

After such a dialogue, Mr. Lorry in his dream world begins to dig the spectre out of the earth; then he comes to himself and opens the window of the coach to let the wind and rain falling on his cheek bring him back to reality. But only for a short time, for before his mind's eye the image of the wasted face appears again, repeating the words, "Almost eighteen years," "I can't say," until Mr. Lorry finally awakes to find himself in the bright light of day and he marvels that a man who has been buried alive for eighteen years is about to be released.

COMMENT

This chapter begins to explain the purpose of Mr. Lorry's trip to France: He is to end an eighteen-year imprisonment of some person, apparently an older man. Lorry imagines his errand as one of literal resurrection, of opening a grave in which a man has been buried alive. Dickens continues to keep the reader in suspense, giving no details of who the prisoner is, what his connection is with Lorry, why he was imprisoned, or what the "Mam'selle" mentioned in the previous chapter has to do with him.

Lorry's descent from the mail coach at the end of the chapter is also presented as a resurrection. He emerges from the darkness into the sunlight, and from a night of the imaginary company of ghosts into a beautiful morning.

Note the repetition of the dialogue between Lorry and the ghost. This is a hallmark of Dickens' style. His flair for the dramatic and the great pleasure he took in public readings of his work probably accounts for this. Repetition helps a listener to remember what he or she hears, and it gives the prose a rhythm and music that impress themselves on the listener.

CHAPTER 4: THE PREPARATION

The coach arrives at Dover and Mr. Lorry takes a room at the Royal George Hotel. After refreshing himself, he comes to the Coffee Room for his breakfast. The staff look at him with interest, having been unable to judge his appearance through his heavy cloak and hat of the journey in the coach; he is a man of sixty, neatly dressed, apparently orderly and methodical, and a little vain, judging by the neatness and quality of his clothing. Although he has the reserved expression of the long-time businessman, his cheeks are rosy and his eyes very bright.

As his breakfast is brought, Mr. Lorry requests a room for a young lady he expects to arrive that day. He adds that the young lady may ask for him by name, or may only ask for a gentleman from Tellson's. The waiter recognizes the name Tellson's, commenting that travelers from the bank often stop at the Royal George. Mr. Lorry agrees that Tellson's is as much a French bank as an English one, although he has not been in France for fifteen years. After breakfast, Mr. Lorry spends the afternoon strolling on the beach of the fishing village of Dover.

In the evening, as he is finishing dinner, the young lady arrives. She is Miss Lucie Manette, a beautiful blonde girl of seventeen. Mr Lorry introduces himself to her, remembering the journey from France fifteen years before, with a small child who was very much like this young girl.

Lucie explains to Lorry that she has received a letter from Tellson's informing her that she must go to Paris to resolve a matter concerning the property of her late father, who died when she was very little. Mr. Lorry finds it difficult to explain his errand, but resolutely treats it as a business matter in an attempt to control his emotions. He explains to Lucie that her father, a doctor from the province of Beauvais, did not die, but was imprisoned for life at the whim of some unknown but powerful enemy. Madame Manette pleaded in vain for his release and shortly thereafter died. Lorry himself took Dr. Manette's young child, now an orphan, to England. Lucie recognizes him and remembers the journey. Lorry then explains that Dr. Manette is alive, although there is no doubt that his eighteen-year imprisonment must have affected him deeply. Lorry's errand is to bring the father and daughter together and escort them to England. Lucie, stunned at this revelation, faints, and a large and fierce woman comes to revive her, accusing Lorry of frightening her darling to death.

COMMENT

This chapter develops the plot. Lorry's errand in France is explained in detail, and the reader is prepared to meet Dr. Manette.

Lorry's personality is fully developed in this chapter. He

is an old gentleman, who is very kind and sensitive despite his attempt to play the role of the detached businessman. His appearance reflects this; his professional reserve and self-control have not suppressed the brightness of his eyes or the rosiness of his cheeks. His long personal connection with the family, as a friend in Paris before Dr. Manette's imprisonment and as Lucie's protector when she was left an orphan, account for his genuine emotions at his first encounter with her in fifteen years.

Lucie impresses the reader with her beauty, youth, and generosity. She makes every attempt to encourage and help Mr. Lorry through his difficulty in explaining his news to her.

Dickens introduces another character at the end of the chapter: a woman who is Lucie's servant. Dickens tells us little about this woman: She is florid, large, fierce and strong (Mr. Lorry thinks at first that she must be a man), and she treats Lucie with great affection, which implies that she has been her servant for a long time.

Lorry explains to Lucie that her father was imprisoned as a result of an unknown, powerful person "filling up blank forms for the consignment of any one to the oblivion of a prison for any length of time." This system was known as the *lettre de cachet* and at one time was responsible for the imprisonment of Voltaire. Any aristocrat could accuse anyone: The accused was never told the identity of the accuser or of the offense, and was given no opportunity to defend himself or herself.

CHAPTER 5: THE WINE-SHOP

Outside a wine-shop in the Parisian neighborhood of Saint Antoine, a cask of wine has fallen from a delivery cart and has shattered on the pavement. A large crowd hurries to the scene to sop up the wine from the street, using whatever means available: hands, cups, even handkerchiefs, which are dipped into a puddle of wine and squeezed dry into the mouths of small children. The scene acquires almost a holiday mood, for all these people who live on dry crusts of bread and a little water suddenly find themselves drinking wine and a spirit of camaraderie prevails—some shake hands, some drink healths to their neighbors, others embrace and dance in the street.

When the wine has all been gathered up, the people return to the cellars and garrets from which they have come. Gloom once again settles down over the street, a gloom more natural to it than sunshine. The signs of hunger and sickness are everywhere. Young children have old faces and grave voices. In the bakeries are a few small loaves of bad bread; in the sausage shop are dog-meat sausages and there are few of these to be seen; in the wine-shops thin wine and beer are served; and everywhere are the faces with hunted looks, with desperation in the eyes, as of some wild beast at bay who turns upon its attackers.

COMMENT

This scene effectively portrays the squalor and deprivation of the French people. The spilling of the wine has a double meaning: It shows that the people cannot be kept much longer from having the necessities of life of which they have been so long deprived; and the red wine running in the streets symbolizes the bloodbath that will in a few years engulf this street and all of France. The people's eagerness to drink every drop of the wine symbolizes their implacable pursuit of every aristocrat under whose sway they have suffered for so many centuries.

The red wine has stained the street and the clothes and faces and hands of the people who have tasted it. One tall citizen writes the word "blood" on a wall with his wine-soaked fingers. The wine-shop keeper, Defarge, has been observing all the activity in front of his shop, and when he sees the citizen Gaspard write "blood" on the wall, he admonishes him, picks up a handful of mud, obliterates the word, and re-enters his shop. Madame Defarge is knitting at the counter and indicates two unfamiliar customers to her husband: an old gentleman and a young lady. Defarge glances at them and then begins to converse with three customers at the bar. All four men address one another as "Jacques." Defarge suggests that they go upstairs to see an apartment that is for rent, and the three customers pay for their wine and leave.

COMMENT

Dickens introduces two more major characters, the Defarges. Dickens describes Defarge as an attractive man, good natured, but also implacable, not likely to be swayed from any purpose. Madame Defarge is a cautious and reserved woman; she says nothing but sits behind the bar watching and knitting. She is observant and misses nothing of what goes on in the wine-shop.

The name "Jacques" comes from "Jacques Bonhomme" (Goodman James), a term contemptuously applied by the nobles to the peasantry who revolted in 1358 against their oppressors. "Jacquerie" ("company of men named Jacques") was the name applied to any revolt of French peasants. In this scene, those who conspire toward the revolution address one another as Jacques.

Thereupon the elderly gentleman, who is Mr. Lorry, leaves his table and whispers a few words to Defarge. Defarge nods and goes out. Mr. Lorry signals to his companion, Lucie, and they, too, go out and meet Defarge in a courtyard nearby. Defarge's face has changed. The good humor is gone and there is no openness about him. Instead, he has now the look of a "secret, angry, dangerous man." Defarge leads Mr. Lorry and Lucie up a long staircase in a building nearby. The decayed refuse on the stair of this ramshackle building poisons the air and increases the agitation that both Mr. Lorry and Lucie feel. "Is he alone?" asks Mr. Lorry. "Alone! God help him, who should be with him?" answers Defarge in a low voice. "Is he always alone, then?" "Yes." "He is greatly changed?" "Changed!" Defarge answers, and mutters a tremendous curse and strikes the wall with his hand.

At last they reach the garret where Dr. Manette is hidden away, and Defarge pauses to take out a key from his coat. Mr. Lorry asks why it is necessary to keep him locked in, and Defarge explains that Manette was so long accustomed to being locked in that he would not understand the door being left open—it would terrify him. As they enter the room of the garret, they see the three Jacques who left the wine-shop just before them. Defarge sends them away, and Mr. Lorry, a bit angry, inquires whether Dr. Manette is put on show. Defarge replies that he does show Dr. Manette to certain men, "to whom the sight is likely to do good." Defarge bangs loudly on a door to an adjoining room, to prepare the gentleman within for a visit, then he opens it, admits himself, Mr. Lorry, and Lucie, and locks the door behind them. As the three stand by the door and their eyes grow accustomed to the darkness, they see a white-haired man, sitting on a low bench, making shoes.

COMMENT

Dickens continues to prepare the reader for the condition in which prison has left Manette. Defarge has duplicated the conditions of the prison, partly because the neighborhood is too poor to provide anything better and partly because Manette has grown so used to these conditions—dark rooms and locked doors—that he would find a change bewildering and upsetting.

Defarge exhibits Manette to the other Jacques in order to keep alive their fury at conditions in France. Manette never sees the Jacques; they look at him through a peephole.

CHAPTER 6: THE SHOEMAKER

Defarge greets Manette, and in a very faint voice he responds. His voice is feeble from lack of use, revealing his long years of solitary confinement. Defarge opens the window to let in more light, revealing Dr. Manette more clearly. He has a hollow, thin face with a raggedly cut white beard and white hair, and large, bright eyes. His tattered clothes reveal the thin, withered body beneath them.

Mr. Lorry steps forward, and Manette looks at him briefly and without curiosity, then returns to his work. Defarge asks him to show the shoe to Lorry, and Manette complies. Defarge asks him to describe the shoe and tell Lorry the maker's name. Manette explains that it is a fashionable young lady's shoe, and gives his name as One Hundred and Five, North Tower.

Lorry recalls himself to Manette as an old banker and an old friend. It becomes clear that Defarge is an old servant of the Manettes. Manette's eyes grow alert suddenly, and then return to their former expression, but Lorry has now definitely recognized his old friend. Lucie comes forward and speaks gently to her father, who is shaken by her strong resemblance to the wife he lost eighteen years ago. He pulls a lock of hair from a rough small leather bag on a string around his neck, and compares it to her hair; he recalls his parting from his wife, and thinks Lucie is she, but realizes she is far too young.

Lucie, deeply affected, tells him that she has come to rescue him and take him back to England. The father and daughter share an emotional embrace, and Lucie urges that they all leave for England immediately. Defarge agrees that this is the wisest course, and Lorry leaves to make the preparations.

As they leave the garret, Manette asks to take his shoe-making bench and tools with him. As the coach leaves Paris, Lorry recalls his earlier imaginary conversation with Manette: "I hope you care to be recalled to life?" "I can't say."

COMMENT

Here the reader sees the terrible deterioration of Dr. Manette, caused by his long imprisonment. Dickens describes him in great detail and with sympathy. He draws upon his long firsthand experience with prisoners and prison life, gained while his father lived in the Marshalsea prison.

This chapter concludes Book One, which is the expository portion of the novel. Dickens has used this book to establish an atmosphere of darkness, violence, suspicion, and danger; to introduce several major characters and establish their relationship to one another; and to place these characters within a specific historical time period.

Except for Lorry's arrival at the Royal George, every scene in the book has taken place in darkness. The journey to Dover occurs during the night; Lorry meets Lucie in a dark room at the Royal George; the neighborhood of Saint Antoine is a gloomy place; Manette's room is so dark the visitors cannot see him at first, and he allows Defarge to open a window to lighten the room only reluctantly. All the characters on the Dover mail coach distrusted one another, even when Lorry identified himself as an ordinary businessman and Jerry as a messenger. The vivid description of the wine running through the streets like blood underlines the violence that pervades Book One. The reader is given several mysteries to wonder about: Why was Manette imprisoned? What is the meaning of Jerry's remark at the end of Chapter 2?

Dickens establishes the Manette family, father and daughter, and connects all the other characters to them and to one another. Defarge is an old servant, and is surrounded by a circle of other characters, his wife and his neighbors and fellow Jacques. Lorry is an old friend and business associate; Jerry is Lorry's messenger.

The time period is clearly established in Chapter 1, as Dickens gives the date of his novel and foreshadows the coming revolution. The sequence of the Jacques' conversation in the wine-shop, Madame Defarge's constant knitting, and the use of Dr. Manette to whet the purpose of the Jacques, as well as the detailed description of the dreadful poverty and suffering of the Parisians and the capricious imprisonment of Manette, arouse the sympathies of the reader on the side of the revolutionaries.

BOOK THE SECOND: THE GOLDEN THREAD

CHAPTER 1: FIVE YEARS LATER

The first chapter of Book Two opens in London with a description of that venerable institution represented by Mr. Jarvis Lorry—Tellson's Bank. Tellson's is an old firm, and things have not changed there very much since its founding. The building in which it is housed is small, dark, and ugly. A customer, in order to do business with Tellson's, must fight his way through an obstinate door, trip down two steps, and find himself before a small counter presided over by an ancient clerk whose hands shake as he holds a check up to the meager light entering through a mud-splattered window to verify a signature.

Tellson's has always been like this and will remain so, for the belief is strong that this is what makes Tellson's a respectable firm and changing it would somehow make it no longer respectable. The same is true of the personnel. "When they took a young man into Tellson's London house, they hid him somewhere till he was old. They kept him in a dark place, like a cheese, until he had full Tellson flavor and blue-mould upon him. Then only was he permitted to be seen, spectacularly poring over large books, and casting his breeches and gaiters into the general weight of the establishment."

During business hours, Jerry Cruncher sits outside Tellson's, waiting for any errand that needs to be run, and when he is out on an errand, his twelve-year-old son, who is the very image of his father, waits in his place.

The scene is Jerry Cruncher's lodgings: a small, two-room apartment in London's East End. Although the neighborhood is poor, the apartment is very neat and clean. It is 7:30 A.M. and Jerry is beginning to stir from slumber, his spiky hair threatening to tear the sheets to ribbons. The first words from his mouth as he awakes are "Bust me, if she ain't at it again!" An orderly looking woman who has been on her knees in the corner of the room leaps to her feet with haste at Jerry's words. In his annoyance at his wife, Jerry throws one of his muddy boots at her. The fact that there is often mud on Jerry's boots in the morning is unusual, for when he returns home from his day's work at the bank his boots are usually clean.

Mrs. Cruncher protests that she was only saying her prayers, but the statement only irritates Jerry more, for he takes particular exception to her saying her prayers for some reason. "What do you mean by flopping yourself down and praying agin me?" "I was not praying against you; I was praying for you," replies Mrs. Cruncher. "You weren't. And if you were, I won't be took the liberty with." Jerry is in a foul mood and remains so through breakfast, accusing his wife of taking the bread from her son's mouth through her "praying against" Jerry. It seems that Jerry's night trade, that mysterious occupation that muddies his boots, has not been going well and there has been no money coming from it. It is clear to Jerry that this state of affairs can be directly attributed to Mrs. Cruncher and her "flopping." For Mrs. Cruncher is not happy with Jerry's second occupation and offers up her prayers that he might see the error of his ways and give it up.

Jerry continues to upbraid his wife right up until the time that he and young Jerry leave for Tellson's Bank, where they take up their positions outside. Shortly after their arrival, Jerry is called inside, for a messenger is wanted. Young Jerry takes his father's place on the stool and mutters to himself, "Always rusty! His fingers is always rusty! Where does my father get all that iron rust from? He don't get no iron rust here!"

COMMENT

Like the prison that held Dr. Manette and the coach that took Lorry to Dover, Tellson's Bank is described as a kind of grave. Young men disappear inside it only to emerge with their personalities completely stifled and their youth gone. It is a dark place, like most of the novel's settings.

As the chapter title makes clear, it is five years after the events in Book One; specificially, it is now March of 1780. Jerry is still Tellson's odd-job man and messenger. Dickens enlarges the picture of Jerry that he began in Book One, Chapter 2. Jerry is a true Cockney, with his own habits of speech and his own peculiar appearance. The black spiky hair on his head is his defining characteristic; Dickens will refer to it many times. Life in the Crunchers' home is rather stormy, but the reader finds the scene between Jerry and his wife very comic. Neither is sufficiently real for Jerry's abuse of his wife to upset or alarm the reader; it is cartoon violence between two caricatures.

Dickens provides a few more clues as to the mystery of Jerry. He has a trade in addition to his job at Tellson's. This trade causes him to go out in the middle of the night and to come home with muddy boots and iron rust marks on his hands. It upsets his wife, causing her to pray for his soul. From the comment Jerry made earlier, it evidently has somthing to do with "recalling to life": If this were to become common, Jerry would suffer.

CHAPTER 2: A SIGHT

Jerry learns that his errand is to go to the Old Bailey, England's famous criminal court, make his presence known to Mr. Lorry who is there, and wait, in case the old gentleman should have need of him. The case being tried on this particular morning involves a charge of treason, for which the punishment is quartering.

Jerry proceeds to the court, makes his presence known to Mr.

Lorry, and settles back in the crowded courtroom to await developments. Seated at the table with Mr. Lorry are two gentlemen in wigs and gowns—one the prisoner's counsel, surrounded by papers concerning the case, and near him another barrister whose whole attention, now and during the course of the trial, seems to be concentrated on the ceiling of the court.

COMMENT

Quartering, also called "hanging, drawing, and quartering," was a dreadful combination of torture and death. The victim was hanged, taken down before he died, cut open, disembowelled, beheaded, and then cut into pieces. This punishment, for which the crowd is eager, extends the atmosphere of violence that pervades the entire novel.

Barristers and solicitors in England, to this day, are immediately recognizable in court for their black robes and white wigs. The Old Bailey still functions as a criminal court. It is in central London, very near the Thames, just across the street from Temple Bar (a gate between the Temple and the Strand, since destroyed), where Dickens places Tellson's. Dickens was a thorough Londoner, and his novels give a detailed and colorful picture of his city.

Dickens arouses the reader's curiosity as to the identity of the barrister who stares at the ceiling. This is his introduction of the hero of the novel, although the reader has no idea of this.

As the prisoner is brought in, all eyes are riveted on him—a handsome man, about twenty-five, obviously a gentleman. The great interest that the crowd shows in this young man is directly attributable to the dire punishment which will be meted out to him—there is no doubt in their minds that he will be found guilty. One can feel the excitement that the crowd is experiencing at the prospect of blood.

The indictment is read. The prisoner, one Charles Darnay, has been charged with spying for the French king against the Crown of England. He has pleaded not guilty.

The prisoner appears calm, though somewhat pale beneath his dark complexion, and his wandering eyes come to rest on two persons seated near the Judge's bench. His attention becomes immediately affixed on these two, so much so that the eyes of the crowd follow his glance. The two who receive so much attention are a gentleman with white hair whose expression makes him at one moment seem old and at another seem in the prime of his life; and with him a young lady, obviously his daughter. Her face is lit with terror and compassion for the accused. A buzzing runs through the crowd, each one wondering who these two are and the word finally reaches Jerry that they are witnesses for the Crown.

COMMENT

Dickens' description of the audience in the courtroom is masterly. He portrays them as a mob, as one collective character, who is eager to see a verdict of guilty followed by a violent execution. The crowd is interested only in the sensationalism of the case, not at all in justice.

Dickens introduces Charles Darnay, another of the story's major characters. The reader tends to assume that he is innocent, since he is described as young, handsome, calm in the face of the threat of execution, and because Mr. Lorry is involved in defending him. Darnay also shows a strong interest in the two witnesses, who are evidently Dr. Manette and Lucie.

CHAPTER 3: A DISAPPOINTMENT

The Attorney-General's approach is designed to make the jury and the crowd feel hatred and resentment toward the accused and pride and favor toward the prosecution's chief witness, one John Barsad. According to the Attorney-General, Barsad felt obliged to turn his friend Darnay in for the good of the country, Barsad being a true patriot, a great public benefactor, and an unimpeachable witness for the Crown. And the jury, being a loyal jury and a responsible jury, "must positively find the prisoner Guilty, and make an end of him, whether they liked it or not." This opening speech stirs the hearts of the jury and the crowd against the prisoner, and the room buzzes over the Attorney-General's speech.

The Solicitor-General's questioning of the witness underlines all the sterling qualities of Mr. Barsad that had already been enumerated by the Attorney-General. Then the Defense Counsel's turn. His questioning of Barsad brings out the fact that Mr. Barsad lives upon his property but he doesn't remember at the moment where said property is; that he has been in debtor's prison a number of times; that he has borrowed money from the prisoner and has not repaid it.

The Crown's second witness, Roger Cly, who was engaged as a servant by the accused, gives testimony to the effect that he became suspicious of Darnay and kept an eye on him. He often noticed Darnay with mysterious lists and saw him show these lists to French gentlemen at Calais and Boulogne. In the course of his testimony, Cly, too, is shown to have an unsavory past and a long acquaintance with Barsad. Cly also claims that he is testifying through motives of sheer patriotism. But the seed has been planted that suggests that neither Barsad nor Cly is to be trusted, that they are probably paid informers in the service of the Crown.

COMMENT

This chapter, which is narrated rather differently from

the preceding ones, shows Dickens at his stylistic best. He reports all the testimony with a wonderful economy of words, characterizing both witnesses for the Crown through their answers to the Defense Counsel's questions. Their testimony for the prosecution is given in one running paragraph apiece; their cross-examinations are given in paragraphs that alternate between question and answer. It is clear to the reader that both are liars. Dickens presents all this information at a rapid pace and maintains the reader's fascination with the trial's outcome.

Mr. Jarvis Lorry is then called to the stand. The prosecutor attempts to persuade Mr. Lorry that Charles Darnay was one of the passengers with him in the coach from London to Dover. Mr. Lorry cannot swear one way or the other, since his fellow passengers were so heavily wrapped up and they avoided any conversation with one another. Lorry has, however, seen the accused before, when they both were on the same packet boat making the return trip from Calais to Dover, across the Channel.

Lucie is called. Her earnestness, her youth and beauty, and her pity are too much for Charles Darnay, and he is shaken as he stands in the prisoner's dock. Lucie explains that she and her father were with Mr. Lorry on the trip referred to above and she spoke with the prisoner on that occasion. She testifies that Darnay told her then that he was traveling under an assumed name on business of a delicate nature and his business might require frequent trips between France and England. She also mentions that he conferred with two French gentlemen up until the moment when the boat sailed for England. She and the prisoner discussed the quarrel between England and the American colonies, and Darnay criticized England's position, adding that "perhaps George Washington might gain almost as great a name in history as George the Third," a statement that does not go down well with the court.

Lucie exhibits great distress throughout her testimony; the prisoner was kind to her on the boat, helping her to shelter her father from the wind and weather of the Channel crossing, and she does not want to repay his kindness by incriminating him.

Dr. Manette is also called as a witness, but he can offer no information, for he has no recollection of what occurred on that Channel voyage five years ago.

The next witness is called on to testify that he saw the accused at a certain hotel in a garrison-town waiting for another person. The witness is quite sure that it was the prisoner that he saw on that occasion. At this point, the barrister who has been staring at the ceiling, tosses a note to the Defense Cousel who, upon reading it, looks with great attention and curiosity at the prisoner. Counsel asks the witness again if he is sure in his identification. The witness says yes. Counsel indicates his fellow barrister and asks the witness if he does not strongly resemble the prisoner. As the barrister rises, stands beside the prisoner, and removes his wig, the witness and the court realize that they are in fact very like one another in appearance, although Mr. Carton, the barrister, is carelessly and untidily dressed, unlike the neat Charles Darnay. Mr. Stryver, the Defense Counsel, uses this resemblance to shake the witness' identification.

Stryver then sums up his case: Barsad and Cly are villains, in cahoots with each other and with the Government; the trips Darnay makes between France and England are indeed business affairs; and, in short, the evidence is very meager and circumstantial. Following which the Attorney-General makes his summation and the Judge makes his charge to the jury. The jury then turns to consider a verdict. At this point Mr. Carton notices that Lucie has fainted upon her father's breast and calls out to the bailiff to assist her out of the room. She leaves with her father, whose face shows that old brooding, pondering look that came upon him while he was offering testimony and had remained there during the trial.

COMMENT

After having introduced him earlier in the chapter, Dickens tells the reader Carton's name. It is clear that despite Carton's absorption in the ceiling of the court-room, he is observant enough both to change the course of the trial by pointing out his resemblance to Darnay and to notice Lucie's distress.

Dickens emphasizes the emotional tie between Darnay and Lucie. She is deeply upset at having to testify for the prosecution, and he is clearly moved by her evident sympathy and pity.

The jurors, after some discussion, announce that they cannot agree and wish to retire for further discussion. The trial has gone on all day and the lamps in the court are now being lighted. The crowd withdraws for refreshment and Mr. Lorry gives Jerry Cruncher permission to do the same, but he charges him to be back when the verdict is announced so that he may take it back to Tellson's. Carton asks Lorry whether Lucie has recovered, and Lorry assures him that she is feeling better. Carton volunteers to tell Darnay this, remarking sardonically that it is wiser for a respectable gentleman like Lorry not to be seen with the prisoner. Lorry is embarrassed but does not argue the point.

Carton calls to Darnay, who answers. Jerry Cruncher follows Carton, "all eyes, ears, and spikes." Darnay thanks Carton for the news of Lucie, and asks him to tell her how sorry he is to have been the cause of her distress. Jerry reflects on how unlike in manner the two men are, despite their physical simi-larity, as he leaves to get some dinner.

An hour and a half later, the jury returns and gives its verdict:

not guilty. Lorry sends Jerry to convey the message "Acquit-ted" to the bank. Jerry mutters that if the message had been "Recalled to life," as it was five years ago, he would have understood its meaning this time.

COMMENT

Note that Dickens titles this chapter "A Disappointment." The final sentence of the chapter refers to the crowd dispersing in search of other prey, since the acquittal has deprived it of the thrill of a gory execution.

Dickens sets up a contrast between Carton and Darnay, emphasizing their physical resemblance in order to heighten the difference in their personalities. Carton speaks carelessly and sarcastically, but is as considerate as he is observant. He is concerned enough about Lucie to ask after her, and perceptive enough to see that it will be difficult for Lorry, as a representative of the bank, to speak in a friendly way to the prisoner. Lorry resents Carton's manner of pointing this out, but does not deny it.

Darnay, in contrast to Carton, is neat in his appearance and straightforward in his speech.

CHAPTER 4: CONGRATULATORY

As the last of the spectators are leaving the courtroom, the Manettes, Mr. Lorry, and Mr. Stryver gather around Darnay, congratulating him on his recent escape from death. Dr. Manette is quite changed from the man we met in Paris. He is alert, intelligent, and upright. Only when that cloud passes over his face, as it still does from time to time, does he revert to his old appearance. But Lucie's loving care has restored him to his former self, and her voice and the touch of her hand banish the cloud when it appears. Charles Darnay kisses Lucie's hand in gratitude and warmly thanks Mr. Stryver for his defense. Stryver is enjoying his success, for it will advance his career.

During the exchange of courtesies, Dr. Manette has been silent, staring at Charles Darnay intently, with a look of dislike, distrust, and fear.

COMMENT

Dickens presents the reader with another mystery to puzzle over. Why does Dr. Manette react to Darnay as he does?

Stryver, who appeared in a purely official capacity in the previous chapter, here appears for the first time as a character. Dickens sums him up wonderfully in one sentence: "stout, loud, red, bluff, and free from any drawback of delicacy" with "a pushing way of shouldering himself (morally and physically) into companies and conversations, that argued well for his shouldering his way up in life." Profound and detailed characterization is not Dickens' great strength as a writer, but he surpasses most writers at drawing a vivid picture of a personality in a few words. Stryver is very appropriately named as well; the trick of matching a character's personality to his name is a tradition of the English novel since its beginnings. Dickens uses this trick for comic characters for the most part.

Mr. Lorry calls attention to Dr. Manette's look, and Lucie hurries him off in a coach. Mr. Stryver withdraws, leaving Mr. Lorry and Charles Darnay together. At this point Carton, who has been standing in the shadows, joins them. No one has made any mention of Carton's part in the acquittal, for only Stryver and Darnay know of it. Carton, who has been drinking, makes another sarcastic reference to Lorry's prior hesitation at speaking to the prisoner. The usually good-natured Lorry is sufficiently annoyed to reply rather sharply, and bidding Darnay an affectionate good night, he leaves them.

Carton takes Darnay to a nearby tavern where Darnay sits

down to a meal while Carton sits opposite him with a bottle of port. Carton speaks of his own disillusionment, lack of friends, and indifference toward being alive. Darnay, still slightly dazed by his ordeal, is at a loss to answer him. Carton suggests Darnay give the toast he is thinking of; Darnay hesitates, but raises his glass to Lucie's health. Carton raises his glass as well, but throws it into the fire rather than drinking. He then praises Lucie, asking insolently if Darnay felt it was worth it to be tried for his life, since the trial gained him so much compassion and pity from her. Darnay changes the subject, thanking Carton warmly for his role in saving his life. Carton shrugs off the thanks as undeserved, and after a moment tells Darnay that he does not particularly like him. Darnay replies politely that he hopes they can part without ill feelings, and leaves Carton over his bottle.

Carton looks at himself in the mirror, bitterly contrasting his slovenly appearance and drunkenness with the manner of his sober and energetic look-alike Darnay. He admits that he wishes they could have changed places; Carton would have liked to have Lucie Manette's regard, as Darnay has had it. "You hate the fellow," Carton tells his reflection, and, swallowing the rest of his wine, falls asleep at the table.

COMMENT

Lucie Manette has made the same impression on both Carton and Darnay. Both are susceptible to her kindness, beauty, and generosity. It is clear, however, that although Darnay has impressed her, she is unaware of Carton's existence.

Dickens uses the conversation between Carton and Darnay to flesh out his portrait of Carton. Carton, who is observant and intelligent, has wasted all his talents and opportunities. He regards the world with indifference, finding no pleasure in anything but good wine. However, Dickens shows that the sight of Darnay and Lucie has affected Carton. Darnay shows him what he might have been, and Lucie's emotion for Darnay shows him what he might have had. Carton has been shaken out of his cynicism.

Once again, Dickens sets a scene in a dark room. The only light in the room is from candles and the fireplace, and the room is full of shadows.

CHAPTER 5: THE JACKAL

Stryver has become a favorite at the Old Bailey and his foot is on the lower rungs of the ladder of success. In the early days of his career it was noted that although Mr. Stryver was a bold, glib, unscrupulous man (all of which characteristics pointed to success), he was not able to focus a cross-examination on the most important points and thus secure an aquittal for a client. Since his acquaintance with Sydney Carton, however, his abilities have improved remarkably, and whatever the case being tried in which Stryver was involved, Carton would be with him in the courtroom. Their colleagues have realized that Carton is entirely responsible for Stryver's success, and they tell one another that although Carton will never be a lion, he is an excellent jackal.

At Stryver's lodgings, Stryver and Carton begin work on the documents for the next day's cases. After wrapping a cold, wet towel around his head, Carton attacks the two piles of papers provided by Mr. Stryver, who sits smoking and daydreaming while Carton works. Both drink heavily throughout the session.

At three A.M. the work is finished, and the two men refill their glasses and sit down to chat. Stryver praises Carton for the day's cross-examinations, and they recall their school days, when their relationship was just the same as now. Stryver was always pushing himself forward, and Carton was always lagging behind. Carton suggests, half-humorously, that his negligent ways are Stryver's fault; Stryver always pushed him so hard when they were students that Sydney adopted a careless manner in self-defense. He then rises to leave, asking for a change of subject before he goes. Stryver raises his glass, toasting "the pretty witness."

Carton loses his good humor, scoffing that she was a mere "golden-haired doll." Stryver looks at him sharply, reminding Carton of his quickness in observing that "the golden-haired doll" was ill in the court. Carton scoffs again: It did not take a magnifying glass for him to see a girl seated two yards from him faint. He drinks Stryver's toast and leaves him.

Carton wanders home through the deserted streets. An overcast day is dawning, and he pauses as a vision of success, happiness, self-denial, and honor rises in his imagination. It fades as he climbs the stairs to his room and flings himself on the bed in his clothes. The sun rises on the sad sight of the waste of his "good abilities and good emotions . . . incapable of his own help and his own happiness."

COMMENT

Stryver and Carton are an unlikely combination at first sight. But these two who have known each other since school days have built a relationship that contributes mightily to Stryver's success as a lawyer. Sydney Carton's quickness and penetrating mind are just what Stryver needs, and the relationship of "lion" and "jackal" gains Stryver a reputation in the law courts and Carton the few necessities of life he requires, although his talents remain unappreciated by all except Stryver. And though Carton can see that his present life is a waste, that his talents might be put to better use than serving as mental drudge to a pompous man like Stryver, he is unable to change his situation.

In this scene, Carton begins to win the regard and

support of the reader. He shows a quick wit and a rue-
ful sense of humor in his conversation with Stryver, and
his long habits of idleness and lack of discipline and
ambition begin to appear as a tragic flaw, as something
that he cannot alter. He is proud, as well; his contemp-
tuous comments about Lucie, which the reader knows
to be the opposite of his true feelings, are made in self-
defense, so that he can avoid discussing her with Stryver.

CHAPTER 6: HUNDREDS OF PEOPLE

It is Mr. Jarvis Lorry's custom to spend Sunday afternoons
with the Manettes in their quiet lodging near Soho Square in
London. It is now four months since Darnay's trial and the
memory of it is gone from the public's mind. Doctor Manette
and Lucie occupy two floors of a house that is otherwise
occupied by a few quiet artisans who are little seen or heard.
The doctor has established a small practice here that provides
him and Lucie with as much money as they need to live.

Lucie and Doctor Manette are not at home when Mr. Lorry
arrives, but since he is quite at home here, he enters the house
and walks through the rooms. In the doctor's bedroom, in a
corner, he sees the disused shoemaker's bench and tools.
"I wonder that he keeps that reminder of his sufferings about
him!" Mr. Lorry says softly. "And why wonder at that," comes
the reply, so unexpectedly as to make Mr. Lorry start. It is
spoken by Miss Pross who, as she served Lucie for so many
years, now serves Lucie and her father. Miss Pross assumes a
proprietary air over Lucie, and she resents the "hundreds of
people" who come to the house to see Lucie. In Miss Pross'
mind, even Dr. Manette is not worthy of such a daughter, but
she could have accepted him if there hadn't been dozens of
others to take Ladybird's affection away from her. In Miss
Pross' opinion, there is only one man on the face of this earth
who is worthy of Lucie—Miss Pross' brother, Solomon.
Although Solomon coldly took all her money and possessions
and deserted her without compunction, she still believes in

his basic worth. This belief remains unshakable, and Mr. Lorry thinks all the better of her for it, although he is well aware that Solomon is worthless.

COMMENT

Miss Pross is the servant who appeared in Book One, when Lucie fainted in the Royal George at the news of her father's condition. She and Mr. Lorry have established friendly relations since that original encounter.

Mr. Lorry and Miss Pross discuss the presence of the shoemaking equipment and find it remarkable that Dr. Manette has never broached the subject of his imprisonment to anyone, not even Lucie, in the years since his release. Miss Pross comments that the subject is a painful one for the doctor and whenever it is approached he instantly changes for the worse. Often in the night Dr. Manette can be heard pacing in his room, tormented by something from the past. On these occasions Lucie goes to him and walks with him until he is composed, but never does he say anything about the reason for his restlessness and Lucie has found it wiser not to hint at it to him. Lucie and Dr. Manette return home from their walk, interrupting the conversation.

After dinner, as they are sipping their wine in the garden, Charles Darnay arrives. In the conversation Darnay tells a curious story he heard while he was imprisoned in the Tower of London before his trial. It seems that an old dungeon that had been covered over for some years was discovered and on one of the corner stones was written the word "Dig." The workmen dug beneath the stone and found a leather bag inside of which were fragments of paper, that had deteriorated so that whatever had been written could never be read. At the conclusion of this story Dr. Manette starts and puts his hands to his head. Lucie is frightened by his look but he recovers himself almost immediately and calmly says that he started because of some drops of rain that had struck him.

COMMENT

Dickens provides another clue to the mystery surrounding Dr. Manette. Since he was a long-term prisoner, and he is so startled by the mention of a prisoner leaving a written record in a cell, the reader can assume that Darnay's story has reminded him that he left a written record in his own cell—a record he had forgotten until this moment.

It is indeed beginning to rain, and the friends go inside where they are joined later by Sydney Carton, and they all sit and look out the window as the storm gathers momentum. Lucie remarks that sometimes, when she has sat before this same window of an evening, she has thought that the echoes of the footsteps in the streets before the house are the footsteps of people who are coming, by-and-by, into their lives. Indeed, many footsteps can be heard rushing and echoing through the storm, and the sounds of lightning and thunder and torrents of rain underline this picture of multitudes rushing down upon them. Mr. Lorry leaves after the storm with Jerry as an escort, commenting that it is "almost a night to bring the dead out of their graves." Jerry replies that he has never seen a night that would do that.

COMMENT

The storm that arrives at the end of the chapter symbolizes the revolution. Carton and Manette observe that it comes slowly and surely, and all the characters listen to the running footsteps of the people trying to escape it.

Mr. Lorry requires Jerry's escort back to Clerkenwell, his own nieghborhood, because he is afraid of being robbed. Once again Dickens sounds the note of violence. Note also Lorry's reference to the dead coming out of their graves, and Jerry's comment that he has never seen such a thing.

CHAPTER 7: MONSEIGNEUR IN TOWN

The Monseigneur of the chapter's title is one of the great lords of the French court. This great lord takes his pleasure at the opera and at private suppers at his estate where it takes four men, besides the cook, to present his chocolate to him. To Monseigneur the world was made for his pleasures and France exists to fill his pocket; there is no doubt in his mind that this will always be the case. In this unreal world exist military men with no military knowledge; naval officers with no idea of a ship; civil officers without a notion of civil affairs. And not far from this palatial mansion, the scene of great suppers and balls attended by gallant gentlemen and fine ladies and catered to by multitudes of servants, is the town full of peasants, scarecrows dressed in rags. And the rustle of fine silks and brocades fans the devouring hunger of the multitudes of the downtrodden citizenry.

COMMENT

Monseigneur is a generic title meaning literally "my lord." It is not a specific rank of nobility such as duke or marquis. Dickens uses the title "Monseigneur" to refer to both the lord who hosts the ball in this chapter and to Monsieur the Marquis.

The ironic tone that Dickens used in the opening chapter is used once again here with devastating effect. The air of unreality, as of wooden puppets performing in a highly stylized drama, pervades the description. The reality of hunger and oppression will, before long, topple the walls of this little theater and break the puppets to bits.

As the grand evening comes to an end and Monseigneur retires, his guests prepare to leave. One gentleman, who has stood a little apart during the evening and has been treated coldly by the Monseigneur, leaves in anger. This gentleman, a Marquis, is about sixty, haughty in manner with a transparently handsome face that has a suggestion of cruelty in it. The Marquis enters his carriage and is driven at breakneck speed through the city.

As the carriage turns a corner, there is a jolt, a loud cry, and the horses rear up and plunge. The Marquis, calmly looking out, says, "What has gone wrong?"

A child has been run down. The child's father is weeping over the body in the street. The people stand around looking cowed—they have been downtrodden so long that there is no hint of rage or hatred in their faces. The Marquis is annoyed at this inconvenience. He takes out his purse and tosses a coin to the child's father. Another man appears on the scene and comforts the weeping father. This new arrival is Defarge, keeper of the wine-shop, and his remarks please the Marquis, who throws him another coin and begins to drive away. Suddenly, the coin is flung back into the coach. The enraged Marquis stops the coach and looks out but Defarge is nowhere to be seen, and in his anger the Marquis does not notice the woman standing nearby staring at him, and knitting. As the coach and its retinue depart, she remains there and knits on with the steadfastness of fate.

COMMENT

This type of incident seems exteme, but Dickens faithfully records a common occurrence in pre-revolutionary France. A lord such as the Marquis did not consider the common people to be human beings: Note that he addresses them as "you dogs." He is more concerned for his expensive horses than for the life of a common child. Aristocrats were far too powerful to concern themselves with a trifle like manslaughter. The fact that the people control their emotions only suggests the strength with which they will break out in time.

Madame Defarge makes another brief appearance in this scene. She says nothing, but looks the Marquis in the face while everyone else avoids his eye. As always, she is knitting.

CHAPTER 8: MONSEIGNEUR IN THE COUNTRY

The Marquis is riding in his carriage through the broken landscape. He passes through a village with poor streets, a poor tavern, and poor people. The coach pulls up at the posting-house gate. The people in the vicinity stop what they are doing to look at the Marquis and he casts his eye at the submissive faces before him. One catches his eye. "Bring me hither that fellow!" he commands. The man is brought before him and questioned. The carriage passed the man on the road and the Marquis noticed that he stared fixedly as it went by. At what? The man, a road worker, explains that he saw a man clinging to the underworks of the carriage, riding along with it, who let go and hurled himself over the hillside before the carriage reached the village. The Marquis sends Gabelle, his bailiff, to look for the man, whom he assumes is a thief.

As the carriage reaches the top of a hill a woman rushes up to beg a favor. Impatiently the Marquis asks what she wants. Her husband, the forester, has died and she asks only that a piece of stone or wood, with his name upon it, be placed over him to show where he lies. For there are many buried under poor heaps of grass and the place will be quickly forgotten when she dies. Before she has finished speaking, the Marquis has driven on his way. As he steps from the coach to the door of his chateau he asks a servant, "Monsieur Charles, whom I expect; is he arrived from England?" "Monseigneur, not yet."

COMMENT

This chapter shows that rural poverty in France is just as severe as the urban poverty of Saint Antoine. The Marquis is as indifferent to the pleas of his own tenants as he was toward running over the child in Paris.

The reader is left to wonder about the man clinging

underneath the carriage. The mention of Charles, who is expected from England, is a surprise; the reader wonders if this is Charles Darnay, and if so, how he is connected to the Marquis.

CHAPTER 9: THE GORGON'S HEAD

The Marquis' chateau is a massive building, all of stone—stone flowers, stone urns, and stone faces of men decorate its facade as if the Gorgon, who in ancient times turned men to stone with a glance, had cast her eye upon the chateau two centuries ago.

The Marquis proceeds up the stone staircase, preceded by a torch bearer. The night is black and there is no sound to be heard save the hoot of an owl disturbed by the light. The Marquis reaches his private apartment upstairs. The rooms are sumptuously decorated as befits such a nobleman, and a supper-table for two has been laid in one of the rooms. The Marquis prepares himself and in a quarter of an hour sits down to his choice supper. As he dines he thinks he notices a shadow at the window, but a servant investigates and there is nothing to be seen but the black night outside. When he is about halfway through his meal, his nephew arrives, revealing himself as Charles Darnay.

COMMENT

The revelation that Darnay is a French aristocrat explains his need to travel frequently between England and France. This is information that is not known to any of the characters who were involved in his defense.

The servant withdraws and the two men converse during their supper. It is clear that deep distrust and enmity exist between uncle and nephew. Indeed, it is clear that the uncle would be content to have Charles out of the way, for it is suggested that the trial of treason was somehow connected with his uncle's efforts. "I believe that if you were not in disgrace with the Court, a *letter de cachet* would have sent me to some fortress indefinitely," says Charles. "It is possible," replies his uncle with great calmness.

It is true that such "instruments of correction" are not within his power, says the Marquis, but then the nobles have lost many privileges.

Charles comments that their name is probably the most detested name in France, but his uncle is not to be softened by such an approach. Charles presses his point. He is bound to a system that is frightful to him, and, to execute his mother's dying wish, to redress the wrongs committed by his family, he seeks assistance and power, in vain. His uncle, however, will do nothing to destroy the system under which he has lived. There is no point in continuing the conversation. Charles renounces his property and France altogether and vows to start again in England under his new name, for England is his refuge. "They say," comments his uncle, "that it is the refuge of many. You know a compatriot who has found a refuge there? A doctor? With a daughter?" Charles answers yes and looks puzzled at the allusion, but the audience is at an end and his uncle bids him good night.

As the sun rises the next day, people go about their tasks as they have done for centuries. The routine of the morning is disturbed by the ringing of the great bell at the chateau and the hurried figures everywhere. The mender of roads gathers with the populace at the fountain in the village to ponder these events, and we hear what has caused all this frenzy. The Marquis has been stabbed to death during the night. Attached to the murder weapon is a piece of paper on which is scrawled, "Drive him fast to his tomb. This, from Jacques."

COMMENT

The Marquis and his nephew cannot see one another's point of view. To Darnay, the common people are people like himself, only less fortunate, and he wishes to use the wealth and power of the estate to help them rather than crush them. To the Marquis, they are not human beings at all; they are a resource to be used as he sees fit. He does not question the system under which he was born. It is this attitude that brought about the revolution.

At the news of the Marquis' death, the reader recalls the man who clung to the carriage on the previous day's journey. The signature Jacques shows that the revolutionaries claim responsibility for the murder.

Note that on the Marquis' death, Darnay automatically inherits the title and the property that he has sworn he will not accept.

CHAPTER 10: TWO PROMISES

It is a year after the death of the Marquis: 1781. Charles Darnay has prospered as a tutor of French and French literature. He spends part of his time at Cambridge University and the rest in London. He spends much of his time with the Manettes, and one summer day when Dr. Manette is home alone, Darnay tells him of his love for Lucie and his desire to marry her.

Dr. Manette reacts with obvious dread and what seems like actual pain. Darnay, thinking that Dr. Manette fears a separation from Lucie if she should marry, assures him that he means to strengthen the bonds between Lucie and her father, not to tear them asunder. Dr. Manette asks whether Charles has spoken to Lucie and if she loves him. Darnay replies that he has not spoken and that he has no reason to believe that Lucie loves him; they have not discussed the matter. Manette tells Charles that if Lucie loves him, he will not stand in the way of their marriage. No matter what he knew against Charles, Manette would not stand in the way, as long as the matter were not Charles' direct wrong and responsibility. Fear and dread haunt the doctor's expression as he utters this promise.

Darnay then tells the doctor that he desires to reveal his true name and the reasons for his being in England. Manette abruptly and decisively prevents him; if Darnay and Lucie decide to marry, Darnay shall tell him on the morning of the wedding. Darnay promises to do this, and leaves before Lucie comes home. As she enters she hears a low hammering sound coming from her father's bedroom. Lucie looks in, gasps in horror, and immediately pulls herself together and goes in. The father and daughter talk for a long time. She comes down from her bed later to look in upon him as he lies asleep. He sleeps heavily, and his shoemaking tools are all in their usual place.

COMMENT

The reader is not surprised at Darnay's desire to marry Lucie; it has been quite clear throughout the novel that they are destined to play the roles of the two young lovers, and that Darnay was in love with her even as early as the trial.

Dickens continues to tantalize the reader with hints about some link in the past between Darnay and Dr. Manette— a link that Darnay is clearly unaware of and that deeply disturbs the doctor. At this point the reader knows that Darnay is a French aristocrat by birth, the youngest member of a domineering family that is hated throughout France by the common people, and that Dr. Manette was imprisoned by some nobleman's request, with a *lettre de cachet* such as Charles described to the Marquis in the previous chapter. The reader begins to guess that Darnay's family may have been responsible for Manette's incarceration.

For the first time since his arrival in England, Manette breaks down completely: Lucie finds him making shoes at his bench. His terror at the thought of losing the daughter so recently restored to him, and Darnay's reminders of his painful past, push him into hiding in his old identity of One Hundred and Five, North Tower. Lucie's love is able to restore him to sanity for the moment.

One year has gone by since Darnay suddenly and unexpectedly came into his property in France. The reader is left to wonder what he has done in regard to it; it is clear that Darnay has settled in England, renouncing the title as he had planned.

CHAPTER 11: A COMPANION PICTURE

Once again Stryver and Sydney Carton have spent the night working on legal briefs. Carton has been laboring every night for many nights in succession to clear up these papers for Stryver before the long vacation. At last they are finished and he pulls off the wet towel from his forehead and begins making another bowl of punch. Stryver then announces to Carton that he intends to marry. After much delaying, during which he criticizes Sydney for his anti-social manner and remarks that he, Stryver, is much more agreeable in a woman's society than Sydney, he announces the name of the lady whom he plans to honor with his proposal of marriage: Lucie Manette. The mention of the name has no outward effect on Sydney's composure except for the fact that he increases his consumption of punch. Because he is a successful man, comfortably off, Stryver feels no doubt that Lucie will accept his proposal gratefully. He then suggests that Sydney should marry— perhaps a widow, with some property. He knows that Sydney has no interest in feminine society, but he feels that his friend should marry "against a rainy day." Sydney promises to consider the matter.

COMMENT

The reader is well aware of the comical incongruity of a match between Lucie and Stryver, and can laugh at Stryver's calm assurance that all he has to do is propose. Stryver's accusations of Carton's indelicacy and insensitivity are ironic in the extreme, since it is he and not Carton who lacks those qualities. Carton has enough sensitivity not to tell his friend that such a proposal is absurd.

Of the three men who have expressed interest in Lucie, two have decided to propose marriage. Carton has said nothing of his intentions toward Lucie, although the reader knows his realistic view of his own wasted life and opportunities and the consequent unlikelihood that he might ask Lucie to share these.

CHAPTER 12: THE FELLOW OF DELICACY

After some thought, Mr. Stryver decides to make Lucie's good fortune known to her before he leaves town for the long vacation. He has not a doubt as to the strength of his case—it is a plain case, and has not a weak spot in it. On his way to the Manette's lodgings to announce himself to Lucie, he passes Tellson's Bank and decides to divulge his intentions to Mr. Lorry who is, as he knows, a close friend of the Manettes. He enters the bank and greets Mr. Lorry in a booming voice that causes the clerks to look up with displeasure at him. Mr. Lorry, discreet as always, greets him quietly in his best business manner and inquires if there is anything he can do for Mr. Stryver. Nothing in a business way, replies Mr. Stryver, for he has come for a private visit and, so saying, he announces his plan to marry Lucie Manette. Mr. Lorry looks dubious, which upsets Stryver.

Finally, after much discussion, Mr. Lorry persuades Stryver to accept him as an emissary, to sound Lucie out on the matter and thus avoid embarrassment to all concerned. Mr. Stryver then bursts out of Tellson's, and it finally dawns on him that there may be some reason for Mr. Lorry's moral certainty that Lucie would refuse him. He determines to take the offensive and put everyone else in the wrong. Accordingly, when Mr. Lorry stops by Mr. Stryver's chamber later in the evening to tell what he has found out, Mr. Stryver seems preoccupied as if he did not know why Mr. Lorry had come by, even though the meeting was prearranged. Finally, Mr. Lorry informs the lawyer that his suspicions were correct and that Mr. Stryver ought not press his suit any further. Mr. Stryver is very off-hand about it, suggests that it was a momentary lapse that made him even consider proposing to Lucie, thanks Mr. Lorry for his good offices, and rushes him out into the night before the gentleman from Tellson's knows what has happened.

COMMENT

This is one of the few unrelievedly comic episodes in the novel. Stryver is not in love with Lucie, nor she with him, and no feelings are hurt. The reader is greatly entertained at Stryver's bluster in Lorry's office, and at Stryver's wise decision to pretend the whole idea was a passing whim when he sees that it will not work out as he had anticipated. The chapter title is taken from Stryver's description of himself in the previous chapter, and is highly ironic.

CHAPTER 13: THE FELLOW OF NO DELICACY

On a pleasant day in August, Sydney Carton once again heads for the Manette house, but this time with an air of resolution. He finds Lucie at home alone at her work. Carton's moodiness has always made her a little nervous of him, but she forgets herself as she realizes from his expression that he is upset about something. She gently asks what is the matter, and he slowly answers that it does not matter; there is no hope for him. His eyes fill with tears, much to Lucie's surprise and sympathy. Carton pulls himself together and explains that he has something particular to say to her; will she listen? Lucie assures him that she will gladly hear him, and Carton confesses that he loves her. He assures Lucie that if she had loved him, he would have been happy, but would also have been too sure of his own disgrace and degredation to take advantage of her love. He asks for no such regard from her. Deeply touched, Lucie asks if she cannot help him without loving him in this way.

Carton answers that she has been the last dream of his soul. The sight of Lucie and her father has reminded him of old hopes and old ambitions that it is too late for him ever to realize. Feeling that she has only made matters worse for him, Lucie is distressed, but Carton assures her that if anyone could have helped him, it would be she. He tells Lucie that this confession is to be the final confidence of his life, and asks her to keep it. She promises to keep it even from those closest to her.

Carton assures Lucie that he will never bring up this subject again, and thanks her for hearing him out. He tells Lucie that however he behaves outwardly, he will always think of her with respect and love, and he makes one last promise; he would do anything, make any sacrifice, for her and for those dear to her, even if his life were at stake. He leaves her with a last "God bless you!"

COMMENT

Carton's consideration for Lucie clearly demonstrates that he is far from the insensitive and indelicate fellow Stryver accused him of being. He knows Lucie will be distressed at what he wants to tell her, and he treats her with great gentleness. Since his first sight of her in the courtroom, Carton's behavior toward Lucie has been chivalrous— the behavior of a lover who expects and receives no encouragement, but who continues to love. The reader is not surprised at Carton's revelation of such deep feelings, since Carton established his interest in Lucie on the night of the trial.

Lucie shows all the qualities that have won the love of every character in the novel: She is considerate, kind, and genuinely distressed at Carton's unhappiness, even though she does not return his love.

Although the idea of noble self-sacrifice is sentimental, the originality of Dickens' two characters lift it above the trite. Carton is a dissipated profligate and a heavy drinker, not at all the type one would expect to feel a disinterested and chivalrous love for a beautiful woman, and Lucie has a strength of character that is atypical for a beautiful blonde blue-eyed angelic heroine. Lucie is the head of her house: Her father leans on her, not she on him.

CHAPTER 14: THE HONEST TRADESMAN

As he sits at his post outside Tellson's, Jerry notices a noisy crowd approaching and he perceives that they are accompanying a funeral. As the crowd draws near, a hearse and a mourning coach, in which there sits a solitary mourner, can be seen, and the crowd is shouting "Spies" and hissing and deriding the man riding in the coach. Funerals at all times hold an attraction for Jerry Cruncher and a funeral that attracts so much attention as this one does excites him greatly. After stopping several members of the crowd to inquire about this funeral, he learns that the deceased is Roger Cly, a spy for the Old Bailey. Jerry remembers Cly from Darnay's trial. The crowd mobs the vehicles, forcing them to stop, and they lay hands on the solitary mourner who just manages to get away after shedding his cloak and hat, which the crowd tears to pieces with great enjoyment.

The crowd commandeers the coach and hearse and proceed to the burial ground where the coffin of Roger Cly is laid to rest, amidst great rejoicing. Looking for new amusement, the mob breaks some windows and maltreats passersby until a rumor that the guards are coming causes them to disperse. Jerry Cruncher, having remained at the churchyard, remembers that Roger Cly was a young, well-made man, and he pays a call on his medical adviser—a distinguished surgeon—on his way back to Tellson's. When he arrives at the bank, young Jerry tells his father that there were no jobs in his absence and, as the bank closes, the two go home to tea.

At home Jerry Cruncher gives one more warning to his wife against her "flopping," and tells her that if his ventures go wrong tonight he will know that she has been praying against him and he will beat her for it just as if he'd seen her doing it. Young Jerry asks to go out with his father but is forbidden to do so.

At about one o'clock in the morning, the elder Jerry opens a locked cupboard and brings forth a sack, a crowbar, a rope and chain, and other fishing tackle of that nature, extinguishes the light, and goes out. Young Jerry, who has gone to bed fully clothed, follows his father out, determined to find out about his mysterious "fishing." Following at some distance, young Jerry sees his father meet two other men and follows them to a churchyard where the three scale the wall. Watching from outside the gate, young Jerry sees the three dig up a grave and, after much labor, succeed in raising a coffin to the surface. The sight terrifies him, and he runs all the way home and scrambles into bed. The next morning the elder Jerry is in a foul mood and he starts the day by knocking his wife's head on the headboard of the bed. "You oppose yourself to the profit of the business and me and my partners suffer. You was to honour and obey; why the devil don't you?" There is not much food for breakfast and Jerry remains out of temper as he and his son set off to Tellson's bank. Young Jerry confides in his father that he would like to learn his nighttime trade, and the older Jerry is pleased to think his son may become a credit to him in the future.

COMMENT

Dickens finally reveals Jerry's night occupation: He and his associates dig up bodies from graveyards and sell them to medical men for scientific experimentation. It is clear now why Jerry objected in Book One to the idea of a man being recalled to life. Dickens does not reveal, however, what went wrong when Jerry and his friends opened Cly's grave.

This episode sounds several of the motifs that run through the novel: mob violence, resurrection, and darkness. The crowd that follows Cly's hearse is celebratory; the people make a festival of the funeral. Cly is followed by only one mourner, and this man runs away at the threat of violence. Jerry's trade is revealed as grave-robbing: He literally digs men out of graves, just as Lorry figuratively dug Manette out of his "grave" in Saint Antoine. The scene in the cemetery takes place in the middle of the night, in secrecy and stealth.

CHAPTER 15: KNITTING

The scene is once again Defarge's wine-shop in Paris. There is an air of preoccupation about the place, and although it is unusually crowded, Defarge is absent. However, no one asks for him, and no one is surprised to see Madame Defarge at the counter, serving the customers and collecting their few coins.

At midday, Defarge enters with the mender of roads who saw the man beneath the Marquis' carriage. As Defarge greets the company, a customer gets up and leaves. Defarge introduces the mender of roads as Jacques and bids his wife to give him some wine. As Jacques drinks his wine and chews on a crust of dark bread that he has carried in his blouse, two more men leave the shop. Defarge then offers to show his guest an apartment that he has for rent. The two men leave the shop, enter a courtyard, and climb a steep staircase to the same garret that Manette occupied after he left prison. The three men who left the shop, the same three Jacques to whom Defarge once exhibited Manette, are there. Defarge introduces them to the mender of roads as Jacques One, Jacques Two, and Jacques Three, Defarge himself being Jacques Four and the mender of roads Jacques Five.

Defarge asks Jacques Five to relate his story to the others. Jacques Five recounts the incident the previous year of the

Marquis' coach and the man hanging beneath it. The man has been sought all this time for the Marquis' murder, and Jacques Five has recently seen him, a captive being marched to the prison that stands on a hill above the village. The assassin and prisoner is Gaspard, whose child was trampled beneath the hooves of the Marquis' horses. All the villagers wonder together what will become of him; will he be reprieved, or tortured and executed?

The other four Jacques listen attentively and exchange dark glances with one another. Jacques Five continues his story: A rumor goes about the village that a petition has been presented to the king saying that Gaspard was maddened by the death of his child and that because of the petition his life will be spared. Jacques One tells Jacques Five that Defarge himself handed this petition to the king.

Jacques Five continues. One Sunday night when the village is asleep, soldiers and workmen come down from the prison, and the workmen dig and hammer while the soldiers laugh and sing, and when the sun rises in the morning, there by the fountain is a gallows forty feet high, poisoning the water. All work stops and the villagers assemble there. At midday, Gaspard is hanged on the gallows and left there.

Defarge asks Jacques Five to wait outside for a moment. When Jacques Five is gone, the other four agree to register the chateau and all members of the Marquis' family to be destroyed. Jacques Two asks Defarge if their manner of keeping the register is safe, and Defarge answers that if his wife kept it in her memory alone, it would be absolutely reliable. As it is, she keeps track of it is a code of stitches in her knitting, and the code is unbreakable by any outsider.

COMMENT

Here Dickens reveals the point of Madame Defarge's knitting, which occupies her so constantly. She is knitting a record of crimes committed by the aristocracy against the common people, and of the judgments and sentences the people have passed on them. Obviously no outsider would ever think of keeping a record in such a way; the register will be entirely safe.

Note the intent to destroy the Marquis' entire family— "extermination" is the word Defarge uses. Charles Darnay, although he has renounced his family name, is a member of the Marquis' family, and in fact the owner of the title and the estate. Dickens is slowly drawing the threads of his plot together.

Once again, a violent scene takes place at night. Under cover of the darkness, the soldiers and workmen erect a gallows, beside the fountain that is the center of village life, both for gossip and for drawing the water necessary for life. The soldiers have deliberately made it impossible for the villagers to draw water; the corpse has contaminated the water, and the villagers are terrified of going near it.

Defarge announces that he will take Jacques Five to see the king and queen at Versailles on Sunday. He feels it is best for Jacques Five to see "his natural prey" in order to whet his appetite for hunting it.

When Sunday comes, the Defarges and the mender of roads make their trip to Versailles in a public conveyance. All the way there, Madame Defarge knits. A fellow passenger asks what she is making. "Shrouds," she replies.

The mender of roads yells himself hoarse cheering the king and queen and court when they enter the salon at Versailles. Later, he regrets his lapse, but Defarge is pleased. "You are the fellow we want. You make these fools believe that it will last forever. Then, they are the more insolent, and it is the nearer ended." Madame Defarge questions the mender of roads.

If he were shown a great heap of dolls and a flock of birds and were set upon them to strip them for his own advantage, he would set upon the richest and gayest dolls and the birds with the finest feathers, would he not?" "It is true, Madame." "You have seen both dolls and birds today," says Madame Defarge. "Now go home!"

CHAPTER 16: STILL KNITTING

The mender of roads returns to his village and the Defarges return to Paris. They stop at the guard station, where Defarge alights and chats with the soldiers and the police there, one of whom he knows quite well. As the Defarges proceed on their way, he tells Madame that a new police spy, an Englishman named John Barsad, has been commissioned for the Saint Antoine quarter. Defarge describes the spy, and Madame Defarge promises to add him to her register in the morning.

COMMENT

John Barsad was the chief witness for the prosecution at Charles Darnay's trial for treason at the beginning of Book Two. With the reintroduction of this character, Dickens brings his plot one step closer to its resolution. The reader begins to realize how tightly organized the novel is; every character in it is essential to the story, and the action of each character apparently has an effect on all the others.

Madame Defarge arranges the accounts in the wine-shop before they retire. Defarge watches but does not interfere. Observing him closely despite her concentration on her task, Madame Defarge comments that he seems tired and faint of heart tonight. Defarge admits that he is depressed: The revolution is a long time coming. Madame agrees, but she is certain that when it does come, it will be absolute and thorough. Defarge wonders whether they will live to see it, and Madame shrugs; if not, they have the satisfaction of having worked to bring it about. She criticizes her husband for his need to see his victim and his opportunity; she can sustain her courage and her purpose without this crutch.

COMMENT

Dickens begins at this point to differentiate between the characters of Ernest and Therese Defarge. It is clear that Madame Defarge has the stronger character; she is more patient than her husband and her energy is more concentrated on their shared aim of overthrowing the current regime. She is an entirely hard woman; Dickens has given her personality no aspect of softness. She observes her husband closely; the reader gets the impression that this is less due to affection than to doubts about his reliability as a revolutionary.

Next day Madame Defarge is at her usual place in the wine-shop, knitting, when a stranger enters. Recognizing him as John Barsad by the description she was given the night before, Madame fastens a rose on her hair, and as she does so, the customers drift out one by one, so casually that an observer would not notice that a signal had caused their departure. Barsad and Madame Defarge exchange a few pleasantries as he sips his cognac. Customers who enter the shop see the rose in Madame Defarge's hair and leave immediately.

While she talks with Barsad, Madame knits his name into her register. Barsad tries to trap her into admitting some discontent with the present order, but she neatly avoids the pitfalls that he lays for her. Barsad mentions that he believes that there is much compassion and anger in Saint Antoine because of Gaspard's execution. Madame replies that she is unaware of such feelings. Defarge enters and Barsad greets him with "Good day, Jacques." Defarge replies that his name is Ernest. Barsad mentions that he is acquainted with the Manettes in England and knows the part that Defarge has played in helping them out of France. Madame informs the spy that since the Manettes' safe arrival in England there has been little word of them. Barsad tells them that Lucie is to be married to the nephew of the late Marquis, known in England as Charles Darnay. This information has a palpable effect on Defarge; his hand is unsteady as he lights his pipe. The spy notes this and records it in his mind. Having scored this one hit, Barsad pays for his cognac and leaves. Defarge is shaken by this new development and hopes that Darnay will not return to France. Madame Defarge is untouched by any such emotion; Charles Darnay will meet the destiny that fate has assigned to him. She rolls up her knitting and removes the rose from her hair, and the wine-shop gradually fills again.

In the evening, the women of Saint Antoine are all to be seen sitting on doorsteps and window-ledges. They are knitting to keep their hands busy—the mechanical work serves as a substitute for eating and drinking, it eases the hunger pangs. Madame Defarge goes from group to group while her husband watches her admiringly: "A great woman, a strong woman, a frightfully grand woman!" Dickens compares her to a missionary who strengthens the faith of his parishioners as he visits them. In the same way, Madame Defarge strengthens the resolution of her neighbors.

COMMENT

Madame Defarge matches her self-possession against the trickery of the professional spy Barsad, and easily gets the better of him. Barsad gains a slight advantage as he sees Defarge's concern at the news of Lucie's marriage. Again, Dickens emphasizes the difference in character between the husband and wife. Although Defarge has no thoughts of abandoning the revolution, he has no wish to bring suffering to the Manette family. Madame Defarge, on the other hand, feels no personal loyalty toward Lucie or the doctor, and would do nothing to prevent Darnay from falling victim to the revolution. As Defarge weakens in stature, his wife gains. Dickens has created an awesome and terrible figure in her.

CHAPTER 17: ONE NIGHT

It is the eve of Lucie Manette's wedding. Lucie has reserved this last evening for her father and they are sitting under the plane-tree in the garden. Lucie is radiantly happy, but she is a little uneasy about her father's reactions to the marriage. He reassures her that her marriage will not injure their relationship. For the first time, Manette speaks of his imprisonment and recalls that he often thought about his daughter and imagined her married and her home full of remembrances of her dear father. This thought comforted him in his long trial. Lucie is warmed by his sincere love for her and they embrace and go into the house.

The marriage will take place the next morning, with Miss Pross and Mr. Lorry as the only guests. The lodgers on the top floor of the house have left, and Darnay and Lucie will continue to live with Dr. Manette. The doctor is cheerful during supper and drinks to the absent Charles. Late at night, Lucie, apprehensive for some reason she does not understand, looks in on her father and finds him sleeping peacefully. Relieved, Lucie returns to her bed.

CHAPTER 18: NINE DAYS

The wedding day has dawned bright and clear. All is in readiness, and Lucie, Mr. Lorry, and Miss Pross are waiting to go to the church; there to wait for Charles Darnay and Dr. Manette who are closeted in the doctor's room. Mr. Lorry remarks on Lucie's beauty and he and Miss Pross both shed a tear of happiness over the coming nuptials. The door of the doctor's room opens and Dr. Manette comes out with Charles Darnay. Lorry notices with concern that Manette's face is deadly pale, which was not the case when he took Charles into the study. They all proceed to the church in two carriages, and soon Charles Darnay and Lucie Manette are married. Everyone returns home for breakfast and then Lucie and Dr. Manette embrace and Charles and Lucie depart.

Mr. Lorry notices that a great change has come over the doctor. The old scared lost look is on his face and he absently clasps his head and wanders into his own room. Mr. Lorry suggests to Miss Pross that they not disturb him. He, Mr. Lorry, must look in at Tellson's, but he will be back shortly, and then he and Miss Pross will take the doctor for a ride in the country.

When Mr. Lorry returns two hours later, he hears a low sound of knocking coming from the doctor's room. Miss Pross, terrified, cries to Lorry that Manette is making shoes again, and that he does not recognize her. Mr. Lorry hurries into Manette's room and speaks to him, but the doctor does not recognize him either. The only hope Mr. Lorry can see is a look of perplexity in the doctor's eyes, as if he were trying to resolve something in his mind. Lorry and Miss Pross agree that Dr. Manette's relapse must be kept secret from Lucie and from all who know him. To this end word is to be given out that the doctor is unwell and requires a few days of complete rest. Miss Pross is to write to Lucie and inform her that her father has been called away professionally; Lucie will therefore not wonder at receiving no letters from him. Mr. Lorry makes arrangements to absent himself from Tellson's in order to look after his old friend. He and Miss Pross take turns watching the doctor at his shoemaking.

The days pass and Mr. Lorry begins to lose hope of his old friend's recovery. At dusk on the ninth evening, the shoemaker's hand has never seemed more nimble and expert.

COMMENT

Dickens provides one more clue to the mystery of the connection between Darnay and Dr. Manette, but continues to leave the reader in suspense. Darnay has told Manette his true identity and his decision to renounce his family and property, and Manette has received the news as a profound personal shock.

CHAPTER 19: AN OPINION

On the tenth morning after Dr. Manette's relapse, Mr. Lorry is awakened by the sunlight shining into the room where he has fallen asleep during his nightly vigil. Going to the doctor's room, he sees that the shoemaker's bench and tools have been put aside again and that Dr. Manette sits reading at the window. At breakfast all is as it was before Lucie's wedding, and Dr. Manette appears not to remember his nine days of oblivion. A chance reference in the conversation makes it clear that several days have passed, and Manette becomes uneasy, trying to recollect the time. Mr. Lorry resolves to discuss the situation with Dr. Manette after breakfast.

Lorry presents the problem to the doctor as if the person under discussion were some other friend. Dr. Manette understands that he is the patient under discussion but is touched by Lorry's sensitivity; Lorry also sees that the doctor understands. Manette asks Mr. Lorry to tell him every detail of the relapse. When Mr. Lorry has done so, Dr. Manette offers his opinion on the case: The relapse was caused by a revival of the train of thought and memory that was the first cause of the malady. An intense association of a distressing nature was recalled, and though he dreaded such a reawakening, his efforts to prepare himself for it had been in vain. But the worst is over, Dr. Manette believes, and only an extraordinary jarring of that familiar chord could renew the disorder. Mr. Lorry is somewhat relieved, but not altogether. However, Dr. Manette's confident belief gives Mr. Lorry the courage to broach another question: Would it not be best to remove the shoemaker's equipment? Is it not a concession to the misgiving to keep the bench and tools? A great struggle is seen taking place in the doctor's mind, but in the end he gives his permission.

When Dr. Manette departs soon after to join Lucie and Charles, as has been previously arranged, Mr. Lorry and Miss Pross, in the night, hack the shoemaker's bench to pieces, burn the fragments in the kitchen fire, and bury the tools and leather in the garden. Miss Pross and Mr. Lorry look and feel like accomplices in a horrible crime as they go about this deed.

COMMENT

Dickens presents another scene of violence and darkness. Mr. Lorry and Miss Pross dispose of the shoemaker's bench and equipment under cover of night.

The reader is impressed by the strength of will that enables Manette to recover from the shock of Darnay's revelations.

CHAPTER 20: A PLEA

Lucie and Charles Darnay have not been home for more than a few hours when Sydney Carton appears at their house to offer his congratulations. Carton takes Darnay to one side and in an earnest manner, unusual in him, apologizes to Darnay for his rudeness to him on the night of his trial, asks him to forget it entirely, and expresses the hope that they may be friends. Darnay assures Carton that he forgot it long ago. Carton then asks that the family allow him to come and go as freely as Mr. Lorry, but without taking any notice of him; that they tolerate his presence occasionally. He tells Darnay he doubts he will intrude on them more than four times a year, but that he would value the knowledge that he would be welcome. Darnay willingly agrees to this request, and they shake hands.

Later that evening, after Carton leaves the house, Darnay speaks of him to the others with mild contempt and condescension. When he joins Lucie in their room that night, he notices a thoughtful frown on her face. He questions her, and she gently rebukes him for his lack of respect and consideration in speaking of Carton. She will not explain how she knows of Carton's good heart and nobility, but she assures Charles that she knows he is a good man and asks only that Charles treat him generously and kindly. She reminds Charles how happy they are together, and how lonely Carton must be. Darnay, touched by her sincerity, readily agrees to what she asks.

COMMENT
As he revealed himself in a new light to Lucie, Carton now speaks with her husband in a manner quite unusual with him. The enmity that Carton once felt for Darnay is now gone and they are now bound in friendship, though Carton will seldom visit the Darnay home.

It has evidently never occurred to Darnay that Carton might have loved Lucie. Carton's sincere gesture of friendship toward a successful rival is sufficient evidence of the good heart Lucie is sure he possesses, but Darnay is not as sensitive as his bride.

CHAPTER 21: ECHOING FOOTSTEPS
The years pass. Lucie gives birth to a daughter, also called Lucie, and the tread of her tiny feet and the sound of her prattling words fill the house with sunshine. Some time later, she has another child who does not live long.

Six times a year at most, Carton joins the family for an evening. On these occasions he is always sober. Carton is the first stranger to whom little Lucie holds out her chubby arms and he remains close to her as she grows up. Stryver meanwhile shoulders his way through the law, dragging his useful friend, Carton, in his wake. Stryver has married a rich widow with three sons, and is fond of telling Mrs. Stryver, over his glass of wine, of the wiles Mrs. Darnay once used to catch him, but he was not to be caught.

The echoes from France are beginning to rumble ominously, and one night in mid-July, 1789, Mr. Lorry arrives late at the Darnay household. He has had a hectic day at Tellson's. The storm brewing in France has caused a run upon Tellson's, for the French customers of the bank are eager to entrust their property to the firm's safekeeping. "That has a bad look," says Charles Darnay, who saw this storm coming long ago.

The scene then shifts to France and the Saint Antoine quarter of Paris. The time has come and the multitudes of scarecrows in the streets clutch for weapons that are handed out to them— blades, bayonets, muskets, powder and ball, axes, pikes— weapons of every description. Every pulse and heart in Saint Antoine is at high-fever beat. It is July 14, a day that is to go down in history as Bastille Day, and the mob, centered around the wine-shop, with Monsieur and Madame Defarge at its head, pushes on to that fortress. The sea rises and with an unearthly roar the battle is joined. Smoke and fire are everywhere, and in the forefront are Defarge, manning one of the heavy guns, and Madame Defarge, rallying the women and carrying an axe with a pistol and knife at her waist.

The women are variously armed, but all are armed alike in hunger and revenge. Gradually the furious living sea wears down the defenders of the Bastille and the fortress is taken! Defarge collars an old prison officer and commands him to lead him to the cell in which Dr. Manette was imprisoned. The turnkey, Defarge, and Jacques Three hurry through the prison, fighting their way through the throngs. Defarge and Jacques Three ransack the cell where they can see the words "A.M., a poor physician," scratched on the wall.

They then retrace their steps and soon are swallowed up by the crowds. The governor of the Bastille has been taken, the man who symbolizes oppression to the thousands gathered there. The governor is borne along through the streets. He is attacked with a rain of stabs and blows, and as he falls dead, Madame Defarge places her foot on his neck and cuts off his head with the knife she has long had ready. The crowd surges on, among the people seven prisoners of the Bastille newly released with seven newly severed heads mounted on pikes.

There is no stopping them now. They are headlong, mad, and dangerous, and they are not easily pacified when once stained red.

COMMENT
Note Defarge's careful search of Manette's old cell. Dickens prepared the reader for this sequence in Chapter 6 of Book Two, when Darnay startled and alarmed Dr. Manette with the story of a prisoner who had left a written record of some sort in a cell.

CHAPTER 22: THE SEA STILL RISES
It is a week after the Bastille has fallen. The scene is Defarge's wine-shop. After the events of the week, no spy dares set foot in the neighborhood: There are too many street lamps nearby that might be used as gallows. Madame Defarge sits with her lieutenant, a woman of the neighborhood who has earned the nickname "The Vengeance" through her bloody participation in the week's events. Suddenly Defarge rushes in, breathless: He has news. Foulon, an old aristocrat who was believed dead, is discovered to be alive. He had once told the starving people that they might eat grass, and afterwards was so afraid for his safety that his friends helped him to stage a mock funeral. Now the ruse has been discovered and the people shout for his blood.

The blood of the citizens begins to boil once again, and The Vengeance runs from house to house arousing the women. The men grab their weapons, and the throng, with the Defarges, The Vengeance, and Jacques Three in front, rushes to the Hotel de Ville where Foulon is being held captive. The crowd is in a frenzy now, and Foulon is led from the building, torn, bruised, and bleeding, begging for mercy. A noose is thrown over a lamp post and Foulon is hoisted up. The rope breaks. He is raised again, shrieking, and the rope breaks again. The third time the rope holds and shortly thereafter Foulon's head is upon a pike. Then the news reaches the crowd that Foulon's nephew, another enemy of the people, is coming into Paris under a guard five hundred strong. He is seized, despite his protection, and in a trice his head and heart are mounted on pikes and the three grisly objects are carried through the streets in a procession. Gradually, calm returns to the streets and the citizens return to their ragged children. Night falls over Saint Antoine. Defarge, as he closes up his shop, speaks to his wife: "At last it is come, my dear!" "Eh well!" answers Madame. "Almost."

COMMENT

Foulon was a real person; Dickens, drawing on Thomas Carlyle's *French Revolution* (see Critical Commentary section below), vividly retells the story of his murder at the hands of the common people. Although the reader is horrified by the ruthless violence of the Defarges and their neighbors, their behavior is to a large extent understandable. Throughout the novel, Dickens has detailed the suffering of the common people and the callousness and selfishness of the aristocrats, arranging the reader's sympathy with the former.

CHAPTER 23: FIRE RISES

A change has come over the village where Gaspard was hanged. The prison overlooking the town does not seem as dominant as it once did—there are fewer soldiers stationed there and their commanding officers are not certain that the soldiers will obey any orders. There are new faces to be seen, rough faces that speak strange dialects. These are members of the Jacquerie, spreading to the four corners of France, stirring up violence wherever they go. One such meets the mender of roads as he works on the highway. They greet each other and sit down to talk. The mender of roads gives some directions to the stranger who then lies down to take a nap. He has obviously traveled far, for his ankles are chafed and bleeding. The red cap he wears identifies him as a member of the Jacquerie. At sundown the mender of roads awakens him and the two men part.

When the village has taken its poor supper, the inhabitants do not retire as usual. A curious whispering has run through the town and all the people turn out of doors and assemble at the fountain. An air of expectancy hangs over them. Monsieur Gabelle, the bailiff of the Marquis' estate, grows uneasy and sends word to the sacristan at the church that it may be necessary to ring the alarm bells by and by. At the chateau, four dark figures assemble in the courtyard. Suddenly, a light is seen in the chateau, and another, and another. Then flames burst forth from the windows. A servant dashes from the chateau and gallops down the hill to the village, calling for help. The alarm bell sounds but no help comes.

The villagers stand about with folded arms, looking at the pillar of flame in the sky. "It must be forty feet high," they say (as high as Gaspard's gallows), and no one moves. The solitary rider gallops up to the prison and asks the officers to help. The officers look at the soldiers who look at the fire and give no orders. "It must burn," they answer.

The villagers, drunk with this evidence of their new strength, remember Gabelle, the man who has always collected their taxes and rent. Surrounding his house, they order him to come out. Gabelle heavily bars his door and retires to his house-top behind his stack of chimneys, resolved if they come for him, to throw himself from the parapet. But the dawn finally comes and the people retire to their homes.

Similar events take place in other villages, on this night and on others, and everywhere the members of the Jacquerie are to be found fomenting unrest, setting fires, and awaking the populace to their new-found power and strength.

COMMENT
The chateau, the symbol of oppression, is burned down and no one lifts a finger to save it. The power of the nobility has greatly weakened. Although the functionar-

ies and soldiers of some villages succeed in bringing the villagers to heel, the local authorities are powerless to put down many of the uprisings.

CHAPTER 24: DRAWN TO THE LOADSTONE ROCK

It is 1792, three years since the fall of the Bastille. In the intervening time, those French aristocrats who were able have left their native land and scattered far and wide, many to England, with whatever possessions they were able to bring. In London, Tellson's Bank is a gathering-place where the nobles can pick up scraps of reliable information from Paris and exchange news of their friends and relatives. Thus, Tellson's serves as a kind of High Exchange, and all inquiries concerning members of the French nobility or events in France are made there.

On a foggy afternoon, Mr. Lorry sits at his desk at Tellson's, talking with Darnay. Mr. Lorry is planning to travel to Paris to straighten out the affairs of Tellson's and to save what records and documents he can. Darnay, concerned for his safety, attempts to dissuade him, but wishes he himself were going, thinking that somehow he might be listened to, and might have the power to persuade some restraint. Lorry sharply rebukes him for even considering such a journey, when he has a wife and child to provide for. Lorry himself, an Englishman with no ties to France, will be quite safe, as will Jerry Cruncher, who will accompany Lorry as his bodyguard and right-hand man.

All around the two men, expatriate French aristocrats boast how they will avenge themselves on the people before long. This empty and absurd buzzing angers Darnay. The buzzing of Mr. Stryver, expounding to the nobles his devices for exterminating the common French people, is especially irritating.

Mr. Lorry's superior brings a letter to his desk addressed to the Marquis St. Evrémonde, entrusted to the care of Tellson's.

Mr. Lorry replies that he has asked everyone there but no one knows of his whereabouts. Charles Darnay notices the name on the envelope and recognizes it as his own. He has told no one his name except Dr. Manette, because Manette made him promise not to reveal it even to Lucie.

COMMENT

Dickens reveals Darnay's real name for the first time; also that Dr. Manette asked Darnay to share this information with no one else. Once again, Dickens stresses the mysterious link between Darnay and Manette.

Several men overhear the name "St. Evrémonde" and comment derisively on the cowardice of the present Marquis, the nephew of the one who was murdered. They criticize him roundly for abandoning his estates to the "ruffian herd." Because of the rioting, mass murders, and other violence committed by the revolutionaries, and because they have heard only the aristocrats' side of the situation, the English are generally sympathetic toward the French aristocrats. Stryver is among the loudest in expressing scorn for the missing Marquis.

Darnay tells Lorry he knows the Marquis and will deliver the letter. Leaving the bank, he opens and reads it. It is a plea for help from Gabelle, who has been imprisoned by the revolutionaries and will certainly be executed unless the Marquis comes to help him. Darnay reflects that despite his good intentions, he has not done all he might have for the suffering peasants on his estate. Although he relinquished the rent and taxes that they had formerly paid to the chateau, he should have finshed the business more carefully, disposing of the property and tying off all loose ends. Instead, Darnay became caught up in his life in England and allowed matters to drift. He realizes that his carelessness is responsible for Gabelle's plight and therefore decides to go to Paris to save Gabelle. Gabelle has written proof that Darnay voluntarily forfeited the estate and title; therefore, Darnay discounts the danger he will be in once he reaches France.

Darnay returns to Tellson's and gives Mr. Lorry a message to take to Gabelle: "He has received the letter, and will come." Darnay plans to leave the following night. That night, he sits up late writing to Lucie and to Dr. Manette, explaining his reasons for going to France and assuring them that he is in no danger. The next evening he bids Lucie goodbye, pretending that he is going out for but a moment; leaves his two letters with a porter for later delivery; and sets out on horseback for Dover and the boat to Paris.

COMMENT

The loadstone rock of the chapter title is a reference to the *1,001 Nights*. It was a mountain whose magical magnetic force destroyed passing ships by pulling out their nails, bolts, and other hardware. This is Dickens' metaphor for the force of events that pulls Darnay back into the dangers of France.

Madame Defarge's comment that Darnay would meet his end according to his destiny is fulfilled. Darnay has taken part in bringing this about, first by his failure to see the disposal of his property through to the end, and now by deciding to return to Paris. Dickens notes that Darnay's certainty of his own safety is a mirage; the reader is prepared for his capture by the revolutionaries. The reader knows, as Darnay does not, of the vow of the Defarges and their associates to exterminate Darnay's family.

Note once again how economically Dickens has used his characters. He might have used a number of devices to get Darnay back to France; he uses a character who has already been established. *A Tale of Two Cities* has far fewer characters in it than most Dickens novels, and each character plays a crucial role in the action.

BOOK THE THIRD:
THE TRACK OF A STORM

CHAPTER 1: IN SECRET

Traveling is difficult in France in 1792. In addition to the normal difficulties of bad roads and bad horses, the traveler must now contend with bands of citizen patriots who stop all travelers, question them, examine their papers, and either turn them back, send them on, or imprison them on the spot as suits their mood.

It becomes clear to Charles Darnay as he proceeds to Paris that there will be no turning back until the Gabelle affair is settled in Paris. As the barriers drop behind him on the road, the feeling strikes him that his freedom is completely gone. Gabelle's letter gets him past all obstacles until he reaches a little town, still a long way from Paris. Here he is stopped again and delayed so long that he takes a room for the night. He is awakened by a local functionary and three armed patriots who wear the familiar red caps on their heads. They tell Darnay that he is to be sent to Paris under an escort and must pay for the escort himself. When Darnay protests, the answer is "Silence! Peace, aristocrat!" which is uttered by one of the patriots. "It is as the good patriot says," observes the functionary, timidly. "You are an aristocrat, and must have an escort."

Darnay sets out at 3 A.M., having paid a heavy price for the two armed guards who ride on either side of him. Despite this ominous sign, Darnay feels no fear as to the outcome of his journey. He is confident that when his testimony and that of Gabelle is heard, they will be freed.

COMMENT

Darnay still does not recognize his predicament. Because he objected to the excesses of the old regime, he is sure he has only to say so and the revolutionaries will trust his word. He utterly fails to realize that peasants and common people who have been victimized for generations would never trust the word of an aristocrat. Even though Darnay is unaware of the episode concerning Gaspard and of the consequent enmity of the Defarges, he is remarkably obtuse in his confidence.

As the three riders reach Beauvais, the streets are filled with people. The mood of the crowd is ominous and many voices call out, "Down with the emigrant." He begs them to hear him. "Emigrant, my friends! Do you not see me here, in France, of my own will?" "You are a cursed emigrant," answers a furious citizen, "and you are a cursed aristocrat!" A decree is mentioned which makes Darnay's life forfeit to the people. When he inquires about this decree, he is told that a decree exists for the sale of emigrants' property; it was passed by the revolutionary tribunal on the day that Darnay left England. There are other decrees planned—banishing all emigrants and condemning to death all who return.

Daylight finds Darnay and his two guards before the wall of Paris. An official comes out and asks for Darnay's papers. As he looks at them he shows some surprise and stares at Darnay with close attention. He withdraws into the guard-house.

While he is gone, Darnay observes that the gate is kept by a mixed guard of soldiers and patriots, the latter being more numerous. While they are free about letting people enter the gate, those wishing to leave are very carefully checked and those waiting in line to be passed often lie down on the ground to sleep or smoke until their turn comes. The man returns and requests Darnay to dismount and he gives to the guards a receipt. The two guards, leading Darnay's horse, turn back from the gate while Darnay is taken to the guard-house, escorted by Defarge.

An officer receives Darnay and questions him. After learning his identity, the officer sentences him to imprisonment in La

Force. Darnay protests vigorously but is told that as an emigrant he has no rights.

As Defarge, Darnay, and the guards go out, Defarge introduces himself to Charles and asks if he is the man who married Lucie Manette. Darnay answers yes; Defarge asks sharply what on earth made him come back to France. Darnay explains about Gabelle and asks Defarge's help in getting word to Mr. Lorry. Defarge refuses to do anything for him; he is the servant of France and of the people. Therefore, he is Darnay's enemy.

As they walk through the streets, Darnay hears an orator speaking to a crowd and learns that the king is in prison. For the first time, he realizes the danger to which he has voluntarily exposed himself. But even now he does not see his position as hopeless, for the mass executions by the guillotine have not yet begun and the frightful deeds that are to take place have not even formed in the minds of those who are to commit them.

Darnay and Defarge arrive at the gate of the prison of La Force. The gaoler grumbles about having to accommodate another prisoner. Defarge departs and Darnay and the gaoler proceed through the prison, many doors locking behind him. The prison is gloomy, dark, and filthy, and the stench is almost overpowering. Finally, they come to a large, low chamber crowded with men and women.

They seem like ghosts as they rise to greet the newcomer. Their manners are refined and elegant, and the ghosts of wit, pride, and frivolity hang over these prisoners as they welcome Darnay to this society of La Force prison. The gaolers in the chamber seem extraordinarily coarse by comparison with those they guard. A gentleman of courtly appearance asks Darnay his name and if he is to be confined "in secret." Darnay answers yes. A murmur of commiseration is heard as the gaoler leads Darnay to another door and the faces vanish behind him.

The door opens on a stone staircase, leading to a low, black door behind which is a solitary cell. It is cold and damp, but not dark. In the cell are a chair, a table, and a straw mattress. After inspecting these objects, the gaoler leaves, telling Darnay that he will be visited and may buy his food, but nothing more. Darnay, feeling as if he has been left for dead, begins pacing about the cell. "Five paces by four and a half, five paces by four and a half," he repeats over and over again, and the words come to his mind—"He made shoes, he made shoes." As he paces faster the roar of the city outside the walls is intermingled with the wail of voices that he knows, rising above the roar.

COMMENT
As his cell door closes on him, Darnay gives way to despair. Lorry referred to Manette's long imprisonment as being buried alive; Darnay feels buried alive as soon as he is locked in.

CHAPTER 2: THE GRINDSTONE
The French branch of Tellson's is located in the Saint Germain quarter of Paris, in a house once occupied by the Monseigneur for whom four men prepared chocolate in Book Two. Mr. Lorry has occupied himself since his arrival in Paris in trying to preserve Tellson's records and to straighten out the tangled affairs of the bank's French customers. On this particular evening Mr. Lorry is sitting in his rooms at the bank. He glances out the window into the courtyard and sees a grindstone that has recently been placed there. Mr. Lorry shivers with a chill of foreboding and closes the blinds. The vague uneasiness that is upon him causes him to decide to go down to examine the bank to see if all is well, when suddenly the door opens and Lucie and Dr. Manette rush in.

In answer to Lorry's amazed questions, Lucie tells him that Charles came to Paris on a mission of mercy and has been taken and sent to prison. At the same moment is heard a loud noise of feet and voices in the courtyard. Dr. Manette goes to look but Mr. Lorry prevents him and rushes Lucie to the back room while he talks with her father. The two men go to the window and open the blind. In the courtyard are forty or fifty men and women gathered around the grindstone. Two men are working it and the rest are lined up to sharpen their weapons on it. All of the men and women are armed, with knives, swords, bayonets, and axes, and all are soaked in blood. Blood is to be seen on the faces and the clothes of all assembled there, and as each finishes sharpening his weapon, he runs off into the street with a frenzied look in his eyes, gone mad with the lust for blood.

"They are murdering the prisoners," murmurs Mr. Lorry, and begs Dr. Manette to hurry down into the throng to attempt to rescue Darnay before it is too late. Dr. Manette, as a former prisoner in the Bastille, has a great influence among the citizens of France, who regard him as their comrade in suffering under the old regime. A moment later he appears in the courtyard and the crowd makes way for him. He speaks to them and they begin to cheer him. Mr. Lorry hears the words, "Save the prisoner Evrémonde at La Force," and sees the crowd, Dr. Manette in their midst, hurry out into the street. Mr. Lorry goes to Lucie to comfort her and to tell her that her father has gone to save her husband. Lucie, under the great stress of the day, falls into a stupor, and Miss Pross and little Lucie, who have appeared, fall asleep on the bed. Twice more during the night, while Mr. Lorry sits watching over his charges, the bell at the gate sounds and a crowd rushes in to the grindstone, and Lucie awakes with a start to be calmed again by Mr. Lorry. As the sun rises, Mr. Lorry looks out into the courtyard once again and sees the grindstone, covered with the red stain that will never be removed.

COMMENT

Dr. Manette's new-found strength and power seem, for a moment, to be capable of obtaining Charles Darnay's release. Dickens has now brought most of his major characters to France.

CHAPTER 3: THE SHADOW

It occurs to Mr. Lorry that he should not imperil the operations of Tellson's by sheltering the wife of an emigrant prisoner under the same roof. At first he thinks of searching out Defarge and asking his advice on finding a safe dwelling for Lucie and her family, but realizes that the Saint Antoine district is the most violent quarter of Paris and Defarge is very likely involved in the revolution. Instead, Mr. Lorry goes out himself and rents a nearby house for Lucie and Dr. Manette. Mr. Lorry immediately moves Lucie and her child, and Miss Pross, to the house and leaves Jerry Cruncher with them to keep them safe.

That evening, Defarge calls on Mr. Lorry. He brings a message from Dr. Manette saying that Charles is safe and that the bearer of this message also has one for Lucie. He tells Mr. Lorry to take Defarge to her. Mr. Lorry and Defarge go out into the courtyard where they find two women waiting, one of them knitting. Lorry recognizes Madame Defarge, in the same attitude as that in which he last saw her seventeen years ago. Her companion is The Vengeance. Madame Defarge is to go with the two men so that she will recognize those whom she has the power to protect should such protection become necessary. Mr. Lorry is slightly dubious about this and begins to be struck by Defarge's reserved and mechanical manner. They go to Lucie's lodgings and are admitted by Jerry Cruncher. They find Lucie alone. Lucie, in her joy at reading her husband's reassuring message, grasps one of Madame Defarge's hands and kisses it, but the hand gives no response but only resumes its knitting.

Lucie is chilled by this utter unresponsiveness. Mr. Lorry explains that Madame Defarge is here to assure Lucie's safety, but his tone lacks conviction as he observes the stony manner of the three visitors. Miss Pross and little Lucie are called in, also to be recognized. Madame Defarge points her knitting needle at little Lucie and speaks for the first time—"Is that his child?" Mr. Lorry answers yes. Lucie instinctively bends to hold the child to her heart as the shadow of Madame Defarge falls on little Lucie.

As the three prepare to go, Lucie grasps Madame Defarge's dress and begs for her help; she wishes to see Charles and to be sure that he is being treated well. Madame Defarge replies that this is not her affair; no doubt Manette's influence will save Charles. Lucie asks for pity; Madame Defarge turns to The Vengeance and recalls that the women of France have for many years seen their husbands and fathers thrown into prison and all their lives they have seen their sisters and children suffer poverty, hunger, sickness, oppression. "Is it likely that the trouble of one wife and mother would be much to us now?" The three go out, and Mr. Lorry tries to comfort Lucie, who is full of apprehension after meeting Madame Defarge. Despite his encouraging words, Mr. Lorry also feels greatly troubled.

COMMENT
Note that Madame Defarge will now be able to identify Lucie and her child by sight. This sequence reminds the reader of her identification of John Barsad. "Extermination of all the race" of Evrémondes includes little Lucie, the youngest member of the family.

CHAPTER 4: CALM IN STORM
After four days' absence, Dr. Manette returns to Saint Germain. In the interim the prisons have been stormed and eleven hundred defenseless prisoners have been slain. Dr. Manette relates his experiences to Mr. Lorry. The crowd took him to La

Force where he found a self-appointed tribunal sitting in judgment. The prisoners were brought before this tribunal and their fate quickly decided: they were either sent out to be massacred, were released, or, in a few cases, returned to their cells. Dr. Manette, having been presented to the tribunal and identified by Defarge, who was a member of the court, pleaded for his son-in-law's freedom and seemed on the verge of having his request granted when, after a hurried conference among the members of the tribunal, he was informed that Darnay could not be released but would be kept inviolate in safe custody. The doctor asked permission to remain there to make certain that Darnay would not be turned over to the bloodthirsty crowd outside the prison. The permission was granted, and Dr. Manette remained there in the prison for three days until the danger passed. As Dr. Manette recounts all this to Mr. Lorry, the latter is struck by the strength and power that is evident in the doctor's demeanor.

Dr. Manette has been appointed inspecting physician of three prisons, among them La Force, and is thus in a position to bring Lucie news of Charles. Darnay is no longer "in secret," but is confined with the other prisoners, and Dr. Manette brings messages from him to Lucie each week. Manette is, however, unable to secure Darnay's release or even to have him brought to trial, for the tenor of the times is against it. The Revolution is still growing, the king and queen have been beheaded, and revolutionary tribunals have sprung up throughout France, ready to deliver innocent people into the sharp jaws of the newly erected guillotine. In the midst of the terror, Dr. Manette walks with a steady tread, cautiously persistent, never doubting that he will save Lucie's husband. But after one year and three months since Darnay's arrival in France, there is no sign that he will be released.

COMMENT

The massacre of the prisoners is historical fact; it took place in the first week of September 1792. Dickens has laid out a very careful timetable for his novel; throughout, he has given exact indications of the passage of time. One year and three months after Darnay's arrival in Paris brings the novel to December 1793.

Despite all this doubt and uncertainty and through the horrors he sees every day, Dr. Manette gains strength. Manette now feels that his eighteen years of suffering were worthwhile; his imprisonment has won him the unquestioning regard of the revolutionaries and is a guarantee that his daughter and grandchild will be safe in Paris. He also feels sure that he can win freedom for Darnay. The father and daughter have exchanged roles; now Manette is the stronger of the two, and Lucie, who has looked after him and protected him for so long, is now dependent on him to protect her.

CHAPTER 5: THE WOOD-SAWYER

Ever since she moved into her new residence, Lucie has seen to it that the household has assumed a normal air; everything in its place, everything done at its appointed time. Little Lucie is taught by her mother regularly, as if they were at home. All is kept in readiness for Charles' homecoming. Such an approach to her situation helps to relieve Lucie's mind. Only at night, sometimes, does she lose her composure and weep on her father's breast, but he reassures her: "Nothing can happen to him without my knowledge, and I know that I can save him, Lucie."

One day, Dr. Manette returns home with the news that there is a certain window in the prison to which Charles can sometimes gain access at three in the afternoon. If Lucie were to stand at a certain spot, Charles could see her there, though she could not see him, and even if she could it would be unwise to give any sign of recognition. Thus, Lucie, the loving wife, begins to go out every day to stand in the appointed place so that her husband might get a glimpse of her. On the third day of her vigil, she is greeted by a cutter of wood whose house is nearby. He makes a gesture towards the prison to indicate that he knows why she is there. "But it's not my business," he mutters and goes on sawing wood. Lucie often meets him there, and sometimes, when she has forgotten herself and gazes up at the prison, she finds him looking at her. But he always mumbles the words, "But it's not my business," and falls to work again.

More than a year goes by and, regardless of the weather, Lucie is at the spot each day. She hears from her father that only occasionally does Charles have the opportunity of seeing her, but on this small chance Lucie would wait out the day for her husband. As she is standing there one afternoon a crowd of people comes around the corner of the prison. Among them can be seen the wood-sawyer, and as she watches the crowd begins to dance the Carmagnole, the grotesque, devilish dance that has been spawned by the Revolution. They surround her, dancing wildly, until finally they pass and leave Lucie behind, frightened and bewildered, as her father appears. He comforts her and tells her that, as there is no one about, she may blow a kiss in the direction of the prison window. She does so and suddenly Madame Defarge appears. She and Dr. Manette exchange a greeting and she is gone.

Dr. Manette tells Lucie that Charles is to be summoned before the tribunal the next day and that he, Dr. Manette, must make certain final preparations before then; in doing so, he must see Mr. Lorry. As Lucie and her father stand in the street, three tumbrils pass, filled with their human cargo bound for the guillotine. When Lucie and Dr. Manette reach the bank, Mr. Lorry comes out to them, agitated, and there is a coat on the chair belonging to some visitor. Mr. Lorry turns to the room he has just left as he repeats to his guest Lucie's words: "Summoned for tomorrow?"

COMMENT
Dickens concludes this chapter on a note of mystery:

Who is Mr. Lorry's newly arrived guest? The reader is aware that only one major character, Sydney Carton, is unaccounted for at the moment.

The wood-sawyer has evidently told Madame Defarge of Lucie's visits to the prison wall, and Madame has come to see this for herself. Lucie is unaware that any show of sympathy with a prisoner of the Revolution is deemed treason. Dr. Manette is no doubt aware of this but believes Lucie and her child to be exempt from any such judgment, because of his own standing among the revolutionaries.

CHAPTER 6: TRIUMPH

The day dawns, and the dread tribunal of five judges, public prosecutor, and jury sits, as it sits every day. The list is read and there are twenty-three names called before the Tribunal today. Only twenty appear, however, for two have died in jail and one has already been guillotined and forgotten. "Charles Evrémonde, called Darnay" is the sixteenth to appear. Of the fifteen before him, all have been condemned in the space of only an hour and a half. As Darnay takes his place before the court, he sees the Defarges sitting in the front row but they never glance his way.

The prosecutor states that Evrémonde is an emigrant and, under the existing decree, all emigrants who return to France are doomed to death. It does not matter that the decree has been passed since Darnay's return. "Take off his head," cries the crowd. The president of the Tribunal then questions Darnay. Following Dr. Manette's advice, Darnay testifies that his title was distasteful to him and that he left France to live by his own industry in England, rather than on the industry of the downtrodden people of France. He has returned voluntarily to save the life of a citizen of the Republic. He submits the names of two witnesses: Gabelle and Dr. Manette. When he explains that Manette is his father-in-law, the crowd begins to sympathize with him.

Gabelle testifies to the truth of Darnay's statement that he came back to save Gabelle's life. Then Dr. Manette is questioned. His popularity and his careful answers make a great impression. He testifies to Darnay's friendship and devotion to himself and to his daughter; that, far from being a friend of the aristocracy in England, he had actually been tried as an enemy by it, for being friendly toward the United States. The jury interrupts the testimony, saying that they have heard enough; they vote unanimously for the prisoner's release. The audience sets up a shout of applause as the president declares Darnay at liberty.

Darnay is overwhelmed by the throng of well-wishers determined to embrace him, these same people who, if the verdict had been different, would have torn him to pieces. As he and Dr. Manette leave the court, the crowd surrounds them, weeping and embracing. It seems to Darnay that everyone who was at the hearing is now on the streets surrounding him. Only two faces are missing—Monsieur and Madame Defarge. The crowd carries Darnay home on their shoulders, while Dr. Manette goes on ahead to inform Lucie. Finally, husband and wife are reunited and the crowd breaks into the Carmagnole and dances away. Lucie embraces Dr. Manette as Darnay tells her that only he could have saved his life. Manette is deeply proud and happy that he has been able to repay Lucie for her care of him since his own release from prison.

COMMENT

Darnay's second trial is an interesting contrast to the first one, early in Book Two. The English mob was as eager as the French one for a conviction and a violent execution. The difference lies in the conduct of the trial. The English trial was properly conducted along the lines of a very old judicial system, with a great deal of testimony, a carefully and formally prepared defense and prosecution, and an appeal on both sides to the reason of the judges and the jury. The French trial is the product of a judicial system in its infancy, which enters the proceeding with a strong prejudice in favor of the prosecution. To secure Darnay's release, Manette appeals to the emotions of the judges and jury; he reminds them of his own imprisonment and that Darnay is connected to him by family.

Note that the Defarges have taken no part in the general celebration at Darnay's acquittal.

This chapter is an excellent study of mob psychology.

CHAPTER 7: A KNOCK AT THE DOOR

Glad as she is to have her husband returned to her, Lucie's heart is not at ease. Every day men and women as innocent as her husband have been fed to the ravenous guillotine, and revenge and hate hang so heavy in the air that fear is always with her for her husband's safety. Dr. Manette, now supremely confident because of the strength he has shown in effecting Charles' release, makes light of Lucie's fears. Both because of their straitened circumstances and the fact that it is wise not to show any conspicuous wealth that would offend the populace, the Darnays keep no servants. Jerry Cruncher, who has been transferred to the Darnay household by Mr. Lorry, and Miss Pross, do all the shopping for the house.

Each afternoon they set forth, Miss Pross with the money, Jerry with a basket, for the market where they make their careful purchases. Since Miss Pross speaks no French, she uses gestures in her bargaining with the shopkeepers, and often gets her price. On this particular afternoon, as Jerry and Miss Pross set out, Miss Pross asks the doctor whether it will soon be safe to return to England. Manette believes it is too dangerous for Charles to try to leave Paris. Miss Pross accepts this news with a cheerful face, despite her longing to return to England. She goes out with Jerry.

As Dr. Manette is telling his granddaughter a story, a knock is heard at the door. Lucie is beside herself with fear as Dr. Manette goes to the door and opens it. Four rough men, all armed and wearing the red caps of the Jacquerie, enter. They have come for Charles Darnay who is to be summoned again before the Tribunal tomorrow. Dr. Manette is shocked. He questions the intruders and learns that the Defarges—and one other—have denounced Darnay. When Dr. Manette asks the identity of the "one other," the man gives him a strange look and replies that he will find out tomorrow at the trial.

COMMENT

As she did in the house in Soho, Lucie hears footsteps. At that time, she sensed that those footsteps belonged to people who would affect her life one day. Here again she hears footsteps, and this time the effect on her life is sudden and decisive.

The Defarges took no part in the celebration over Darnay's release in the previous chapter. They have evidently laid plans to denounce Charles to a point where Manette's influence will be insufficient to save him. Dickens leaves the reader eager to discover the identity of the third person whom the guards refuse to name to Manette. Note, however, that the guard assumes that Manette knows his identity, and looks at him oddly when Manette asks for the name.

CHAPTER 8: A HAND AT CARDS

Jerry Cruncher and Miss Pross are threading their way to the marketplace, unaware of the calamity that has just taken place at home. Having made a few small purchases, Miss Pross remembers that they must buy some wine. They go to a shop nearby that seems quieter than most. There are a number of people in the wine-shop in various attitudes—drinking, smoking, playing dominos, reading a newspaper. As Miss Pross and Jerry enter the shop, a man rises from a table in the corner and starts toward the door. He comes face to face with Miss Pross who takes one look at him, screams, and claps her hands. Jerry stares at the man in amazement. The crowd is on its feet in a moment, expecting that someone has been murdered. Miss Pross addresses the stranger as her long-lost brother Solomon. He urges her not to call him that—it might prove fatal to him—and asks who Jerry is. Miss Pross introduces them, and Solomon asks why Jerry stares at him so: Does he think he is a ghost? Jerry evidently does think so but says nothing. The three leave the shop together.

COMMENT

Solomon Pross has been mentioned twice before, as the brother who stole Miss Pross' money and left her destitute, but whom she still believes to be the best of brothers and a fine man. Note that Jerry recognizes Solomon, although Solomon does not recognize Jerry and this is the first the reader learns of any acquaintance between them.

Solomon is not at all happy to have met his sister, and he tries to send her away and not endanger his life by her chatter, but Miss Pross asks only for a kind, friendly word from the brother whom she has not seen for so long. As Solomon grudgingly gives it to her, Jerry Cruncher interrupts to ask whether his name is John Solomon or Solomon John. Solomon eyes him suspiciously. Cruncher persists. He remembers Solomon from England, but in England Solomon's name was John, and Pross was not his surname. Jerry cannot recall what this was, however, until he hears a voice behind him utter the name Barsad. Jerry immediately remembers this name and turns to the speaker—it is Sydney Carton.

COMMENT

Dickens gives the reader a great surprise—John Barsad, the paid informer and spy, is Miss Pross' brother! Although Dickens has carefully laid the groundwork for several other revelations, dropping hints and clues along the way (such as Jerry's nighttime occupation), this particular moment has not been foreshadowed.

Carton tells them that he has just arrived in Paris and has seen no one but Mr. Lorry, with whom he agreed not to visit Dr. Manette and Lucie until all was well with Darnay. He commiserates Miss Pross on having a Sheep of the Prisons (that is, a spy for the gaolers) for a brother. Barsad starts to deny the accusation, but Carton explains that he saw him coming out of the prison of the Conciergerie, clearly remembered him from Darnay's long-ago trial in England, followed him to the wine-shop, and listened to enough of his conversation with another man there to be quite sure of his accusation. He then suggests that Barsad go with him for a talk—perhaps to Tellson's offices, where they can speak privately. Barsad hesitates, but agrees to go with him. The three men will escort Miss Pross home and then go to Tellson's. Carton gives Miss Pross his arm, and as she pleads with him not to harm her brother, she becomes aware of a new manner in him—he is alert, purposeful, and very kind to her.

Lorry receives the three men at Tellson's, and Carton presents Barsad to him. Lorry recognizes but cannot place him, until Carton reminds him of the trial for treason. Carton then tells Lorry that Barsad is also Miss Pross' brother, and that Darnay has been arrested again. Lorry is shocked and dismayed, but he sees from Carton's expression that he has something in mind, and does not give way to his emotions.

Carton tells Lorry that although he hopes Dr. Manette's influence may save Darnay again, he doubts it—Manette's not having known of the arrest nor being able to prevent it have alarmed him. Carton plans to play cards for the stake of a friend in the Conciergerie, and that friend is to be Barsad.

Barsad scoffs, "You need have good cards, sir," and Sydney,

asking first for a glass of brandy, looks over his cards. First, Barsad has given a false name to his employers, the French Republic. Second, Barsad formerly worked for the English government, which is sympathetic to the aristocrats and therefore an enemy of the Republic. Third, the French would immediately assume, on hearing of his past, that Barsad was a double agent, still in the service of England. Carton also has an ace in his hand; he threatens to denounce Barsad to the Section Committee immediately. He then ironically invites Barsad to look at his own cards.

Barsad is well aware of the dangers of his position. As a spy, he is not safe anywhere; at any time, the wrong word to the wrong person might be fatal to him. Nor has he forgotten his conversation with Madame Defarge and her ominous glances at him as she knitted. However, he attempts to escape Carton's trap. He mentions his sister, but Sydney assures him that relieving Miss Pross of her brother would be an act of great kindness and respect on his part.

Carton then recalls a fourth card in his hand. He asks Barsad the name of the friend and fellow-spy with whom Carton heard him talking in the wine-shop. Barsad replies that Carton does not know the man. Carton frowns; he is sure he remembered his face. Then he remembers the name—Cly, the servant who testified against Darnay at the Old Bailey. Barsad relaxes and smiles, explaining to Carton that Cly is dead—Barsad can produce his death certificate.

At this moment, Lorry, who has listened attentively to the conversation, sees the spiky shadow of Jerry's head move against the wall as Jerry steps up to the table and asks what became of Cly's body—Jerry and two others know for certain that Cly's coffin was filled with earth and stones, not a body. Carton and Lorry, amazed at this interruption, ask Jerry to explain. Jerry answers evasively that this is not the time—the important point is that Barsad knows perfectly well that Cly was never in that coffin. Carton turns back to Barsad, detailing for him the strength of this last card—if the Select Committee knew that Barsad was in touch with a spy for the aristocracy who has mysteriously come to life again, they would execute him.

Barsad throws in his hand. He will hear Carton's proposal but reminds him that there is little he can do without risking his own life. Carton asks to speak to him in private, and they leave the room together.

COMMENT

With great skill, Dickens extends the metaphor of a card game through the last half of the chapter. Despite the seriousnes of the issue and the danger with which the characters are surrounded, the metaphor of a game is entirely appropriate to the battle of wits and bluff between Carton and Barsad.

This scene reveals the mystery of Jerry's annoyance and bad luck the night he and his friends dug up Cly's coffin. Jerry had promised to deliver a healthy male body and found nothing in the coffin but dirt and rocks. This moment is a triumph of plotting, and it shows how carefully Dickens worked this novel out before he began writing. For Carton to be able to win the card game with Barsad, it was necessary for Jerry to have been a grave-robber, and hints about Jerry's grave-robbing began in Book One.

Carton's demeanor in this chapter is entirely different from his manner throughout Book Two. His is no longer idle, careless, and detached; he has taken control of events and evidently has a plan in mind to save Darnay. Although Dickens withholds the details from the reader, he has provided clues earlier in the novel: Carton believes his own life has no value; he swore to Lucie that he would sacrifice his life to keep a life she loved beside her; and he and Darnay strongly resemble one another physically. Those who read a good deal know that look-alike characters in novels always exchange identities sooner or later.

CHAPTER 9: THE GAME MADE

While Carton and Barsad confer in the next room, Mr. Lorry looks at Jerry Cruncher with considerable doubt and mistrust. Mr. Lorry tells Jerry that if he has practiced an unlawful occupation, as the evidence seems to show he has, then he is not to expect that Mr. Lorry will keep his secret from Tellson's when they return to England. But Jerry, in a long and involved speech, persuades Mr. Lorry of his good intentions and promises to reform when they return home. He tells Mr. Lorry that the constant executions in France have given him a good deal to think about, and he makes the remarkable offer that he will become an ordinary grave-digger, thus making amends for his unlawful digging. Mr. Lorry relents and drops the subject.

COMMENT

Although Jerry is more a caricature and a personality than a fully developed character, he is an entirely original creation. His lengthy speech in his own defense is a wonderful blend of practicality, contrition at being caught, and zeal to change his ways. This speech is nearly the last comic moment in the novel.

Carton and Barsad return to them, and Barsad leaves immediately. As Jerry leaves, Carton and Lorry sit together by the fire. Carton tells Lorry that he has ensured one visit to Darnay, to take place after the trial, if he is convicted. Lorry is disappointed, but Carton reminds him that Barsad will do nothing that will put his own life at risk. Lorry, distressed and deeply concerned, begins to weep, and Carton speaks to him with a gentleness and respect that comfort Lorry and also surprise him, since he has never seen Carton's nobler side. In this moment, the two men become friends and allies.

Carton asks Lorry not to mention his presence in France to Lucie, or the access to Darnay that he has secured. Lucie will not be able to use that access to see her husband, and she might distress herself by jumping to incorrect conclusions about it. Lorry promises to keep the secret. Carton asks if Lorry will see Lucie that night; he knows she will welcome her old friend, since she must be in despair. Lorry answers that he will go to her as soon as he parts from Carton. Carton cannot help asking how Lucie looks, and on hearing the answer "Anxious and unhappy, but very beautiful," lets out a long, grieving sigh. Lorry looks at him, puzzled at this reaction, and thinks how much the cloud on Carton's face reminds him of the faces of the many prisoners he has recently seen.

Shaking off the mood, Carton asks whether Lorry's business in Paris is concluded. Lorry replies that it is; he had intended to leave Paris immediately. They fall silent; Carton then asks a question or two that cause Lorry to look back over his seventy-eight years, throughout nearly all of which he has been a man of business, and to think humbly and gratefully of Lucie and little Lucie's love for him. Carton asks hesitantly whether Lorry's childhood seems very far off in his memory, and Lorry answers that it did twenty years ago, but now it seems close; his memories of his childhood and his mother are very clear. Carton understands, but Lorry reminds him that he is young. Carton shrugs off the subject of himself, and, helping Lorry on with his coat, offers to escort him to Lucie's house.

COMMENT

This conversation shows Carton in a softened mood, to which Lorry readily responds. In their only previous conversation, Carton spoke sarcastically and Lorry was offended; in this scene, they speak as intimate frinds speak, allowing silences in the conversation and talking about the matters closest to them. Note that Carton's mind is preoccupied with the subject of the end of a life and the regard the dead hold in the hearts of the living.

After leaving Mr. Lorry, Carton meets the wood-sawyer and passes a few words with him. The man obviously takes great delight in watching the executioner at work. The wood-sawyer is surprised to hear that Carton is English; he speaks like a Frenchman.

Carton walks on and stops at a chemist's shop where he purchases two packets of certain chemicals. The chemist warns him to keep the two separate because of their effect when mixed. Carton takes the packets and goes out. He wanders through the city, for he has no desire to sleep. He muses on the deaths that day at the guillotine, for the next day's victims and all the others to come, and the words of the Anglican funeral service come into his mind: "I am the resurrection and the life, saith the Lord; he that believeth in me, though he were dead, yet shall he live; and whosoever liveth and believeth in me shall never die." Carton finds comfort in these words and repeats them to himself throughout his night wanderings.

COMMENT

Dickens' description of Carton's long walk through Paris is wonderfully evocative of the experience of a solitary walk at night in a busy city, where everyone else has company and a place to go and only the walker is alone. Dickens also sounds, once again, the motif of resurrection that is one of the themes of the novel.

The next day, Carton attends Darnay's trial. From his place in the crowd, he can see Mr. Lorry, Dr. Manette, and Lucie. The same determined patriots are on the jury, prominent among them a man with a craving on his face—Jacques Three of Saint Antoine.

The hearing begins. The prosecutor announces that the accused is openly denounced by Ernest Defarge, Therese Defarge, and Alexandre Manette. A great uproar follows the reading of Dr. Manette's name. Manette rises and indignantly denies that he has accused Darnay, but the president of the Tribunal silences him.

Defarge is called and recounts his former life in the service of Dr. Manette, the occasion of the imprisonment, the doctor's later release and his own part in tending to the doctor after his release. The Vengeance interrupts the hearing with praise for Defarge's part in the taking of the Bastille. The crowd is clearly with him. Defarge continues his story: On the day the Bastille fell he proceeded to the cell where Dr. Manette had formerly been imprisoned, and in searching it found a scrap of paper, the handwriting on which proved to be Dr. Manette's. Defarge presents the paper to the president of the Tribunal and the order is given that it be read.

CHAPTER 10: THE SUBSTANCE OF THE SHADOW

Dr. Manette's prison diary was written with a rusty iron point dipped in scrapings of soot and charcoal mixed with blood, written in great secrecy and hidden away in the chimney. He writes in 1767, the tenth year of his imprisonment, in the hope that someday the paper will be found and read.

On a cloudy December night in 1757, the doctor was walking by the Seine when a carriage pulled up near him. Someone called his name. He answered, and two men got out of the carriage and came up to him. They assured themselves that he was the Dr. Manette whom they were seeking. They then asked him, in a peremptory manner, to enter the carriage. He had no choice but to do so. The carriage sped off with its three passengers and finally stopped at a solitary house. After opening a gate to let them in, one of the men locked it behind them. As they entered the house, the doctor noticed that the two men were twin brothers.

The doctor was led to an upstairs room, where a beautiful girl of about twenty lay on the bed, her arms bound with a gentleman's scarf bearing armorial devices and the letter E. Over and over again, she uttered piercing shrieks, repeat the words, "My husband, my father, and my brother!" count up to twelve, and say "Hush!" The two brothers stood by while Dr. Manette examined the girl, and they answered his questions impatiently and haughtily. After he administered a sedative, provided by the brothers, he was told that there was another patient.

Surprised, the Doctor followed the brothers to a nearby room where lay a young peasant boy, no more than seventeen, mortally wounded by a sword-thrust. It was clear that he could not live much longer. When Dr. Manette asked the elder brother how this had happened (Dr. Manette used the term "elder brother" to indicate the one who seemed to be in authority), the reply was, "A crazed young common dog! a serf! Forced my brother to draw upon him, and has fallen by my brother's sword—like a gentleman." There was no pity in the voice but only disgust that a gentleman had had to deal with a mere peasant, and annoyance that he had to die there, so inconveniently.

The boy, with his last ounce of strength, raised himself up to tell his story to Dr. Manette. His family were poor peasants and they were miserably oppressed by the two brothers as peasants were oppressed throughout France by the nobility. His sister had recently married a man who was ill and whom she cared for and tended. The younger of the two brothers happened to see her one day and was attracted to her. He asked his brother, who bore the title of Marquis and controlled the land, to lend her to him. The Marquis was agreeable, for it was the prerogative of the nobles to help themselves to any peasant women who struck their fancy. But the virtuous girl refused and bore great hatred for the younger brother. They then began working her husband day and night so that he might persuade his wife to surrender to the younger brother. But he did not give in and one day, at noon, he sobbed twelve times, once for every stroke of the bell, and died on his wife's bosom. The wife was then taken away by the two brothers for the pleasure of the younger. When her father learned of her fate, his heart burst. The girl's brother had then hidden away his younger sister to save her from a similar fate and had climbed into the house where he challenged the younger brother who had been forced to unsheathe his sword and mortally wound him. Then, after telling his story to Dr. Manette, the young boy cursed the two brothers and all their race, and fell back, dead.

The doctor returned to the girl who was still shrieking and repeating the same words. At last she sank into a lethargy and Dr. Manette, in composing her as she lay on the bed, discovered that she was pregnant, and he lost all hope for her. She lingered for a week, then she died without revealing her family name, exactly as her brother had done. Upon learning the news of her death, the Marquis turned to his brother and said, "I congratulate you, my brother." They then offered Dr. Manette a gold coin, which he refused, and warned him that all that he had seen and heard was to remain a secret. They left without another word and Dr. Manette was driven home.

The next morning, Manette found the gold coin in a box at his door. He decided to write a letter to the Court Minister detailing the affair, in order to ease his mind, although he was quite aware of the immunity of the nobles and suspected that nothing would come of it. Accordingly, he wrote the letter, without mentioning names, and later delivered it himself. After he had finished it, he was told a lady was waiting to see him. She identified herself as the wife of the Marquis Saint Evrémonde, the elder brother. She knew the story of the doctor's adventure and wished somehow to make whatever amends she could. She asked Dr. Manette if he knew the address of the younger sister so that she might do something for her but, unhappily, he did not. She was a good, compassionate lady, unhappily married, but determined to do what she could. As the doctor saw her to the door, there was a young boy waiting in the carriage for his mother. It was for his sake, she told the doctor, that she wished to make amends for the sins of the Saint Evrémonde family, for she continued, "I have a presentiment that if no other innocent atonement is made for this, it will one day be required of him." She then drove off.

That evening, a man rang at the doctor's gate and was admitted by the doctor's servant, Ernest Defarge; he informed the doctor that there was an urgent case that required his attention. When Dr. Manette left the house, he was bound and gagged. The two brothers then stepped out of the darkness and identified him with a gesture. The Marquis then held the doctor's letter before him and burnt it with the flame of a lantern. Not a word was spoken. Dr. Manette was then brought to his cell, One Hundred and Five, North Tower, where he remained buried for eighteen years. Dr. Manette closed his document with the words, "And them and their descendants, to the last of their race, I, Alexandre Manette, unhappy prisoner, do this last night of the year 1767, in my unbearable agony, denounce to the times when all these things shall be answered for. I denounce them to Heaven and to earth."

As this narrative is finished, a bloodthirsty sound arises from the court. The jury unanimously convicts Darnay to death the following morning.

COMMENT

Dickens finally reveals the reason for Manette's imprisonment and the link between Manette and Darnay—it is Darnay's family, the Saint Evrémondes, who had Manette thrown into the Bastille. It is now clear why Manette was so uneasy about Darnay's marriage to Lucie, about Darnay's long-ago story of the prisoner who left a memoir in his cell, and about Darnay's never revealing his real name.

The despicable behavior of the two Saint Evrémonde brothers in Manette's story was far from unusual for French aristocrats in the eighteenth century and earlier. The *droit de signeur* entitled any nobleman to take any woman on his estate before her marriage; this custom was the basis of Beaumarchais' play (and Mozart's opera) *The Marriage of Figaro.* In Book Two, Dickens established that the Marquis believed in the system under which he had lived, and this look back at his youth demonstrates this attitude even more clearly.

The Marquise Saint Evrémonde's fear for her son's future turns out to be well-founded. The boy in the carriage outside Manette's house was Charles Evrémonde, later called Darnay. The reader pictures the scene—thirty-five years earlier, the young boy Ernest Defarge, the young Dr. Manette, the child Charles, all meeting for the first time.

CHAPTER 11: DUSK

As the court empties, Lucie and Charles share a last embrace before he is returned to his cell for the last time. Dr. Manette is mad with anguish but Darnay comforts him and asks his forgiveness. As Darnay is led away, Lucie faints and Sydney Carton steps up and carries her to a waiting carriage. He, the unconscious Lucie, Mr. Lorry, and Dr. Manette proceed to Lucie's lodgings where Carton carries her up to her room tenderly. He bends over, kisses her cheek, and whispers something. Little Lucie many years later is to reveal his words: "A life you love."

Carton urges Dr. Manette to intercede once more with the officials although there is little hope in the present situation. Dr. Manette assures Carton that he shall, and will know the results by dark. Carton says that he will come by Mr. Lorry's at nine to learn of them. As Mr. Lorry sees Carton to the door he says, "But he will perish; there is no real hope." "Yes, he will perish; there is no real hope," repeats Carton and walks out with a settled air about him.

CHAPTER 12: DARKNESS

Sydney Carton pauses in the street, not certain what he should do while waiting until the nine o'clock meeting. He decides that it is best to show himself, and after dinner and a nap he proceeds to Defarge's wine-shop. The Defarges, Jacques Three, and The Vengeance are the only people in the shop as he enters. He orders a glass of wine in fumbling French and Madame Defarge is quick to perceive the physical resemblance between him and Darnay. His apparent inability to speak much French deceives them, and they do not attempt to speak quietly. Carton, pretending to be absorbed in his newspaper, hears that Madame Defarge wishes to destroy Dr. Manette, Lucie, and little Lucie, as well as Darnay. Defarge, remembering his years as a servant of Dr. Manette and the compassion of Lucie for her husband, demurs, and wishes them to be spared. Madame Defarge does not share his hesitation. She tells her companions that she was the sister who was hidden away by the boy before he crossed swords with the brother of the Marquis. The dead sister and brother were her sister and brother, and she will stop at nothing to wipe out all traces of the family of Evrémonde to avenge her own family.

COMMENT

Once again, it becomes clear to the reader how carefully every element of this novel was worked out. Madame Defarge is not simply an automaton devoted to the Republic for its own sake; she has a personal motive, revenge on those who destroyed her family.

Carton pays for his wine and goes out. At nine o'clock he appears at Mr. Lorry's. Lorry is in a state of agitation—Dr.

Manette has not come back. At ten he goes out to see about Lucie while Carton waits for the doctor. At twelve Mr. Lorry returns and still no sign of Dr. Manette. Then they hear him on the stairs. As he enters they see that all is lost—the doctor is wild-eyed and unkempt, his coat is half fallen off, and he asks piteously for his shoemaking tools and bench.

Carton and Lorry persuade Manette to sit down by the fire, and as he huddles there miserably and tries to warm himself, Carton takes Mr. Lorry some way into his confidence. Mr. Lorry has already made arrangements to leave France. Carton removes a paper from the doctor's wallet: it is a pass out of Paris for Dr. Manette, Lucie, and little Lucie. He gives this to Mr. Lorry along with his own pass and instructs Mr. Lorry to keep the papers safe and to make everything ready for a departure the next afternoon. Lucie is in danger of denunciation by Madame Defarge, for sympathizing with a prisoner of the Republic. The wood-sawyer will testify to her afternoons outside the prison walls. Mr. Lorry catches the flame of Carton's manner and listens to him attentively, promising that all will be arranged. He learns from Carton that they are all to be in the coach the next afternoon, and when he, Carton, arrives to occupy his place in the coach, they are to make for England as quickly as possible. After seeing Dr. Manette home, Carton bids goodbye to Mr. Lorry and breathes a farewell to Lucie as he looks up at her lighted room.

COMMENT

The pace of the novel has been so swift and the action so violent that few first-time readers will pause to figure out what Carton has in mind. However, it is clear that he does not expect to see Lucie again; he bids her farewell before leaving.

Note that until she and her husband read Manette's prison diary together in their shop, Madame Defarge had never told him of her past. She is clearly a woman of tremendous self-control.

CHAPTER 13: FIFTY-TWO

In the prison of the Conciergerie, fifty-two convicted prison-ers await execution. One of them is Charles Darnay. Alone, in his cell, he has resigned himself to meet his death with cour-age. He writes a tender letter to Lucie telling her of his prom-ise to her father and of his own ignorance of the role his family had played in the doctor's imprisonment, and begging her to comfort her father in his anguish. He also writes a letter to Dr. Manette, confiding his wife and child to his care, and a letter to Mr. Lorry, settling his business affairs. It does not cross his mind to write to Carton.

Shortly after one o'clock in the morning, Darnay hears foot-steps and turns to see Sydney Carton being let into his cell. Darnay is dumbfounded. Carton reassures him: He has not been imprisoned but has been allowed in to bring a message from Lucie. He orders Darnay to do everything he says; it is all a request from Lucie, and Carton has no time to explain. Carton quickly commands Darnay to change clothes with him. The bewildered Darnay complies, but doubtfully. He protests that they cannot escape—they will both die if they attempt it. Carton ignores these comments and orders Darnay to sit and write as he dictates; Darnay does so. Carton dictates a brief message that the reader knows is directed to Lucie, reminding her of his long-ago promise and urging her not to grieve for him now that he is keeping it.

As Carton speaks, he removes his hand from his coat and brings it close to Darnay's face. The drug that he purchased earlier takes effect. Darnay's hand trails off and in a moment Carton's hand is over Darnay's face, his arm around his waist. The struggle lasts but a moment: Darnay lies insensible on the floor. Carton puts the paper in Darnay's coat, calls to Barsad, and orders him to take Darnay out. On the way into the prison Carton had pretended to be weak and faint in order to pre-pare the guard for the condition of the man Barsad is to lead out. Carton tells the spy to take Darnay to the waiting coach and to remind Mr. Lorry of his promise. Barsad calls two gaolers and they take the unconscious Darnay out. The door closes behind them and Carton listens for the sound of an alarm, but there is none.

A short while later, Evrémonde is called and Carton and his fifty-one fellow prisoners are assembled in a large, dark room. As he waits, a young seamstress comes up to him who was imprisoned with Darnay in La Force. Carton has shaken his long hair loose from its ribbon, so his face is somewhat concealed, but when the little seamstress looks up at him she realizes he is not Darnay but a stranger who is dying for his sake. She asks to hold his hand until they are parted at the foot of the guillotine.

Meanwhile, a coach reaches the outskirts of Paris and a guard demands the papers of its occupants. Mr. Lorry identifies each: Dr. Manette, Lucie, little Lucie, "Sydney Carton," and himself. The coach is permitted to go on; the first danger passed! Lucie is anxious about pursuit but the road behind is clear. At a posting-house their horses are changed and a citizen calls to them. Are they discovered? But no; he wishes simply to learn the number of those condemned today. The coach continues toward the Channel and safety as Darnay begins to emerge from his drugged unconsciousness and, thinking he is still in the cell with Carton, to ask what he has in his hand.

COMMENT

Carton carries out his promise that he would do anything, even give his life, if to do so would ensure Lucie's happiness. This chapter assures the reader that even if Carton is discovered, the others are safely across the barriers and on their way to England.

Note that Carton has told no one of his plans; Lorry and the others will recognize Darnay immediately when he is brought to the coach, but by then they will be unable to stop Carton. Carton is well aware that none of them would have allowed him to die in Darnay's place had they known that was his intention.

Throughout Book Three, Carton has appeared at his most appealing and attractive. He has finally found a purpose and has fulfilled it decisively. The reader admires his strength of purpose, alertness, intelligence, and willing sacrifice.

CHAPTER 14: THE KNITTING DONE

Madame Defarge meets with Jacques Three and The Vengeance, not at the wine-shop but at the shed of the wood-sawyer. After the day's executions they are to meet in Saint Antoine, and the wood-sawyer will testify against Lucie and her father. Madame Defarge decides to go to visit Lucie, for undoubtedly she will utter something against the Republic in despair at losing her husband and this will provide additional evidence. Madame Defarge gives her knitting to The Vengeance, tells her to save a chair at the executions, and goes out to Lucie's lodgings. She walks with a confident tread, a dagger and pistol tucked into her belt, an absolute lack of pity in her heart.

Meanwhile, Miss Pross and Jerry are preparing their own departure. Mr. Lorry has arranged for them to leave later, in a lighter carriage, so that they can overtake Lorry's carriage and make arrangements for fresh horses on the road, thus expediting the escape and saving precious time. Miss Pross and Jerry are both free to leave Paris at any time, and are therefore safer than the occupants of Lorry's carriage.

In the midst of this preparation, Jerry Cruncher vows that he will never do it again (referring to his grave robbing), and will henceforth permit Mrs. Cruncher to "flop" all she pleases. And all the while Madame Defarge draws nearer.

It is agreed that Jerry will get the coach and Miss Pross will meet him elsewhere so as not to arouse suspicion with two coaches leaving from the same place. Jerry goes out to make the arrangements and Miss Pross begins to bathe her tired eyes in cool water. Suddenly she looks up and cries out, so startled that she knocks the bowl of water over and watches it flow across the floor to meet the feet of Madame Defarge.

Miss Pross realizes that the open doors will suggest flight to Madame Defarge, so she closes them and takes up her position in front of Lucie's chamber. Madame Defarge demands to see Lucie, and Miss Pross refuses to let her. Neither woman understands the words of the other, but each perceives the other's intentions. Something tells Madame Defarge that her quarry has flown and she opens three of the doors; all is in disorder and there is no one there. But she must make certain. She once again demands that Miss Pross let her look in the room before which she stands. Miss Pross refuses. Madame Defarge makes for the door and the two women struggle. Madame Defarge reaches for her pistol; Miss Pross sees it and strikes at it. The gun goes off and the lifeless body of Madame Defarge falls to the floor.

COMMENT

This confrontation is perhaps the most remarkable scene in the novel. Madame Defarge and Miss Pross somehow understand one another, although neither can speak the other one's language. Both women have such strong personalities that they display their intentions to one another with perfect clarity. As they struggle, Miss Pross realizes that she is stronger than her adversary, and she proudly refers to her English heritage several times during their battle. "You shall not get the better of me. I am an Englishwoman." "You wicked foreign woman; I am your match." This is both comic and touching.

Miss Pross puts on her bonnet, locks the door behind her,

pulls herself together, and rushes out to meet Jerry. Her face is scratched and her hair torn but fortunately her veil hides most of this evidence. She meets Jerry at the cathedral and they drive away. As they ride along the streets of Paris, the awful rumble of the carts taking the fifty-two condemned souls to the guillotine can be heard. But not by Miss Pross. For the exploding pistol has deafened her, and she is never to hear anything again.

COMMENT

Dickens' decision to rob Miss Pross of her hearing is inexplicable. It puzzles the reader entirely. Deafness from close proximity to a pistol shot is improbable, and it serves no purpose of plot or theme. One wonders if it is an attempt at humor that backfired, but it seems unlikely.

CHAPTER 15: THE FOOTSTEPS DIE OUT FOREVER

Six tumbrils carry the day's victims to the guillotine. The prisoners ride silently through the streets, some observing the people in the streets, some sunk in despair. There is great curiosity among the people to see the aristocrat Evrémonde. He is standing in the third tumbril with his head bent down, talking to a young girl. The carts reach their destination. In front of the guillotine are a number of chairs occupied by women, knitting. Among them is The Vengeance, who is puzzled at Madame Defarge's absence.

As the tumbrils begin to empty and the heads begin to fall, the knitting women count. One! Two! As the crowd of victims begins to thin out, the little seamstress, who has been holding Carton's head for comfort, thanks him for his kindness, and then it is her turn. She kisses Carton and mounts the scaffold. The blade falls: Twenty-Two. Carton recalls the words from the Anglican burial service as he mounts the scaffold. Twenty-Three.

That night, Parisians comment to one another that Evrémonde went to his death with a peaceful look on his face. If Carton had been able to write his last thoughts before he died, they would have been something like this: "I see a beautiful city and a brilliant people rising from this abyss. . . . I see the lives for which I lay down my life, peaceful, useful, prosperous and happy. . . . I see that I hold a sanctuary in their hearts and in the hearts of their descendants, generations hence. It is a far, far better thing that I do, than I have ever done; it is a far, far better rest that I go to than I have ever known."

COMMENT

Although such an extreme sacrifice for a woman one has loved and lost is both sentimental and melodramatic, Dickens' skill moves the reader rather than inviting ridicule. G.K. Chesterton said that one would have to have a heart of stone to read the death scene of Little Nell in Dickens' *The Old Curiosity Shop* without laughing, but no such impulse to humor occurs here. Throughout the novel, Dickens has endeared Carton to the reader, giving him the very recognizable flaw of a lack of purpose and discipline, but also endowing him with generosity, loyalty, consideration, and a quick, observant intelligence. Carton neither harms nor endangers anyone (other than hostile witnesses) during the course of the novel, and at its end he restores life and happiness to several people. Because of the reader's affection for Carton, his death provokes admiration for his heroism.

Carton's thoughts on the scaffold underline again Dickens' mastery of style. Every sentence of these paragraphs, except the final one, begins "I see. . . ." This parallel structure gives Carton's unspoken speech a strong cadence and rhythm and makes it linger in the reader's memory. It also closes the novel as it began, with a paragraph of parallel clauses all beginning with the phrase "it was." The final sentence has its own double parallel structure and repetition. The speech is a very well written piece of rhetoric.

CHARACTER ANALYSES

SYDNEY CARTON

Carton is the most fully fleshed-out character in the novel. When the reader first meets him, he is rude, somewhat arrogant, sarcastic, and drunk. Chapter by chapter, Dickens slowly develops his character, until by the end Carton has won the reader's love and admiration.

Carton's faults are acknowledged and presented as part of his character. He is almost the tragic hero of drama; a heroic, noble man whose one character flaw destroys him. Carton's flaw is a lack of purpose and discipline, which have led to a disgust with life and an absolute indifference to his own fate.

Carton's first appearance in the novel, at the Old Bailey, show the reader that despite his manner, he is observant and considerate. He points out his own resemblance to Darnay, thus undermining much of the prosecution's evidence, and he is the first to notice that Lucie has collapsed and to get help for her. Soon after this chapter ends, the reader finds out that Carton, not Stryver, planned the entire defense and prepared all the questions for the cross-examination. His plan to save Darnay in Book Three and his decisive manner of carrying it out again underline his quick intelligence.

Carton's conduct toward Lucie is entirely chivalrous. He makes no attempt to win her love, believing that he would eventually make her unhappy, and he rarely visits her house, since he does not wish to make her uncomfortable. His confession of his love, with its complete lack of expectation of any return, makes a sentimental scene, but the reader has begun to feel a great affection for him and accepts the scene in the spirit in which it was conceived.

Carton's hand at cards with Barsad is one of the most tightly constructed and exciting episodes of the novel. The reader sees what Carton might have achieved had he not lacked discipline and purpose, and cheers at his masterful handling of the spy. From this scene until the end of the novel, Carton maintains his purpose, appearing decisive, alert, and strong. The thoughts that go through his mind as he spends his penultimate night wandering through Paris make a striking impression on the reader. Because he is such an appealing character, Carton's sacrifice for unfulfilled romantic love appears noble rather than trite.

MADAME DEFARGE

Madame Defarge inspires fear in everyone who meets her. Although she says very little, her glance is so hard and so searching that few people can look her in the face. Throughout most of the novel she is as implacable a revolutionary as the Marquis Saint Evrémonde is an implacable aristocrat. Late in Book Three, Dickens gives her a personal motive for revenge against a particular family; she is determined to exterminate those who destroyed her own family. Her self-control is so great that she has never told her husband the story of those deaths. Madame Defarge is entirely without pity. Her coldness makes Lucie shiver, and the reader also shivers. Madame Defarge is one of Dickens' most striking creations.

LUCIE MANETTE

Lucie strikes us immediately as a gentle, unassuming young woman with great inner strength. It is this strength that saves her from being the conventional beautiful blonde innocent heroine of so many romances and adventure stories. Lucie is the central figure in her family and her small social circle, and all the people around her look to her as the most important person among them. The "golden thread" of the title of Book Two is the thread Lucie spins about all those in her circle, binding them all together as a family.

At the beginning of the novel, Lucie is determined to nurse

her father back to health and happiness, and she never wavers from this aim during the course of the story. Until he is welcomed as a comrade by the revolutionaries in Paris, Dr. Manette is entirely dependent on his daughter for his peace of mind. Lucie cures him of his feeble wandering with love, consideration, and gentleness—the same qualities with which she treats all the characters in the novel.

Mr. Lorry looks on Lucie as if she were his own daughter. Miss Pross adores her for her beauty, charm, and kindness. Both Darnay and Carton fall in love with Lucie. Darnay is lucky enough to win her love, and Carton is ennobled by his friendship with her. Even the boorish Mr. Stryver is affected by her beauty and charm, so much so that he decides to propose marriage despite Lucie's lack of material advantages.

When Lucie learns of her husband's imprisonment she rushes to Paris to be with him, disregarding the danger. Her behavior during his long incarceration and trial bear out our first impression: Lucie is a loving, faithful wife who shows strength and determination during the awful months of fear and uncertainty, and her courage never fails from the beginning of the book to the end.

DR. ALEXANDRE MANETTE

Dr. Manette is introduced in Book One, a trembling ghost of his former self after eighteen years in solitary confinement. During the five years that pass between Book One and Book Two, Lucie's love and devotion restore him to much of his original vigor. Manette has an extraordinarily strong will, which is able to subdue his leftover fears, lost memories, and concerns for the future. Only on very serious occasions, such as Darnay's revelation of his real name, does Manette break down. His nervous collapse after the reappearance of his prison diary and Darnay's subsequent conviction appear to the sympathetic reader to be permanent, although Carton's final speech hints that he will recover.

Dr. Manette gains strength in Paris, where he is accepted by the revolutionaries as a comrade and fellow victim of oppression. Using the power this regard gives him, he saves his son-in-law, thus giving his daughter back her husband. Manette is overjoyed to make this return for all the loving care Lucie has given him since they were reunited in Book One.

JERRY CRUNCHER

Jerry Cruncher, odd-job man at Tellson's and "resurrectionist" on the side, is a true London cockney. Along with Miss Pross and Mr. Stryver, Jerry could not possibly have been conceived by anyone other than Dickens. He is most thoroughly characterized in his apologia to Mr. Lorry on the subject of his grave-robbing, which is a marvelous mixture of practicality, guilt, remorse, and evasiveness. Jerry is both amusing and endearing; he enlivens every scene in which he appears. He is more a personality than a person, but he is a much finer achievement than the wooden and unconvincing Darnay.

JARVIS LORRY

Mr. Lorry, though at no time does he seem to be a terribly important character in himself, actually has a great deal to do with the development of the plot. It is he who tells Lucie about her father and goes with her to France to bring him back to England; it is he who brought Lucie from France originally; it is he who gives Darnay the fateful letter that draws him to Paris; and it is he to whom Carton turns to carry out part of the scheme to rescue Darnay. Actually, at most of the crucial turnings of the plot, Mr. Lorry is present and participating. The man of business, who once describes himself as a "mere machine," several times serves as a machine to advance the plot. But Dickens' skill covers the mechanics of development, and we think of Mr. Lorry not as a mechanism but as a warm, cherubic man of affairs who is loved and respected by all those who come in contact with him.

CHARLES DARNAY

Darnay is more a plot device than a character. He is the link between the Defarges and the Manettes, and he provides the reason for Lucie, the doctor, Miss Pross, and Carton to travel to Paris in Book Three. Despite Darnay's service to the plot, Dickens does very little to flesh out his personality. He is young, handsome, well-intentioned, honest, and not very sensitive to the world around him. Darnay saw the conditions in France before the Republic, and his remark to the Marquis in Book Two shows that he was well aware of the hatred and resentment of the common people. Nevertheless, and despite the obstacles he encounters on his way to Paris in Book Three, he does not recognize his own danger until he is actually imprisoned. He is too conscious of his own honorable motives to understand that the revolutionaries want revenge, not justice.

Darnay also displays a lack of sensitivity toward other people. He speaks contemptuously enough of Carton, a man whom he knows has saved his life, that Lucie is moved to scold him gently. He is also insensitive to the fragile state of Dr. Manette's health and sanity, never thinking of the effect his joining the family and his revelations of his membership in the French nobility might have on a man who was imprisoned for so long. Nor does Darnay consider his family when Gabelle's letter shows him that his honor is at stake; despite the distress he should know they will feel, he abandons them without a second thought. In all these cases, his real fault is simply that his honor and honesty prevent him from being very wise. Dickens portrays him as a thoroughly conventional young man, and the reader can only wonder why Lucie loved him rather than the appealing Sydney Carton.

MR. STRYVER

Stryver appears in only a few scenes in the novel, but he leaves a striking impression on the reader. Dickens etches him on the reader's mind in a few sharp, telling sentences. He is loud, pushy, and ambitious, without the talent to achieve his ambitions. However, he is intelligent enough to compensate for his lack of talent by hiring and harnessing the talent of his old friend and schoolmate Sydney Carton.

ERNEST DEFARGE

Defarge is basically a good man who has seen much sadness and injustice about him and who has determined that he will one day set matters to rights. The description of him as "good-humored looking on the whole, but implacable-looking, too," well suits him, for when the Revolution is set in motion he is its mainspring. Although he believes in the Revolution, he hesitates momentarily when he realizes that people with whom he is personally involved, Lucie and her father, may become its victims. However, the hesitation is only momentary. Defarge does not oppose his will against that of his formidable wife.

MISS PROSS

Miss Pross is a typical down-to-earth, no-nonsense, English-woman. She is good-hearted and decent, despite an outward gruffness. She has found her place in life as Lucie's maid, and she fusses over Lucie as if she were her own. For her Lady-bird, Miss Pross would do anything, which she proves in her encounter with Madame Defarge. Up until this encounter Miss Pross has always seen the good in everybody, even in her worthless brother Solomon, from whom she asks only a kind word despite his mistreatment of her. But even without understanding Madame Defarge's words, her intuition tells Miss Pross that this is a thoroughly evil woman, bent on destroying everything that Miss Pross holds dear, and this belief gives Miss Pross the strength to conquer her adversary.

THE MARQUIS SAINT EVRÉMONDE

The Marquis Saint Evrémonde, the uncle of Charles Darnay, is a product of the aristocratic system that prevailed in France for hundreds of years before the Revolution. He is neither better nor worse than any of his noble brethren, and Dickens makes it clear that he could have chosen any one of the noble lords at court and the resulting portrait would have been much like the one of the Marquis Saint Evrémonde. He is handsome, well-dressed, always poised and self-assured; and there is a look of cruelty in his face. He cares for nothing but his own position and pleasures. The death of a child beneath the wheels of his carriage causes him no distress: He is only annoyed because his journey has been delayed. He really believes that Gaspard is at fault for letting his child be run down and the Marquis feels that he is being very beneficent in bestowing a gold coin upon the bereaved father. This coldness and obliviousness is further portrayed in the conversation between the Marquis and Charles Darnay. It is clear that the Marquis would have no compunction in eliminating his nephew if it were in the power to do so, blood ties meaning as little to him as the misery of a father whose child has just been killed.

CRITICAL COMMENTARY

INFLUENCE OF CARLYLE

The inspiration for the writing of *A Tale of Two Cities* came from Thomas Carlyle, the great Scottish historian and essayist. Dickens, like so many of his fellow countrymen, was deeply impressed by Carlyle's book, *The French Revolution*, and he kept it within easy reach on his bedside table. With the exception of a small volume, Mercier's *Tableau de Paris*, all of Dickens' historical knowledge of the French Revolution and of the city of Paris during the Revolution came from Carlyle. According to Kitton (see Bibliography), Dickens, "in order to be accurate in writing *A Tale of Two Cities* asked Carlyle to lend him some of the authorities quoted in *The French Revolution*. Carlyle, as a joke, sent all his reference volumes, comprising about two cart-loads of books." We are told that Dickens read them faithfully.

Dickens and Carlyle were quite different types: Carlyle, a noted scholar, collected and sifted many documents to produce his great work; Dickens, a self-educated man, gathered his material through careful observation of the people and events about him. It was Dickens' genius that he could write about a city and an event about which he knew next to nothing and produce such a stirring, believable portrait of the time. Dickens was well aware that the condition of the peasants was not as bad on the eve of the Revolution as it had been earlier in the century. But taxes were still inequitable (the nobility and clergy were exempt), and the nobles were even trying to revive feudal dues that had lapsed. Carlyle carefully analyzed the first stirrings that led to the eruption years later, and the theory of historical inevitability is closely bound up with his name: Given a certain set of circumstances, certain results can be predicted, as in the case of the abuses that led to the Revolution.

NEW STYLE OF WRITING

In writing *A Tale of Two Cities*, Dickens employed a style quite different from that which he had used for his earlier novels. In the earlier works there is a profusion of characters and incidents; here the characters and incidents are few and each event is included in the story because it must be there and each event has a definite place in the structure of the plot. There is no leisurely rambling in the writing, no irrelevant details, nothing episodic. The writing is tight, concentrated, and stripped of all inessential material.

Thus, *A Tale of Two Cities* is a novel of plot rather than character. The emphasis is on narrative rather than dialogue. This makes for a gripping tale, one that holds the reader's interest until the last page. But in using this technique, an author assumes the risk of having his characters appear lifeless and lacking in individuality. And in *A Tale of Two Cities* Dickens does not always avoid this pitfall. The only fully fleshed out character in the novel is Sydney Carton.

CRITICISM OF CHARACTERS

Charles Darnay is a mere shadow of a character. Lucie is the conventional pretty heroine, a good daughter, wife, and mother, but her courage and inner strength, exemplified in her care and support of her father, save her from being a type. Stryver, though he is on stage for only a short while, is well sketched. Dickens always regarded men in politics or law with a jaundiced eye, and Stryver conforms to Dickens' image: an insensitive, pushing vulgarian who forges ahead in a world that Sydney Carton can make no sense of or get along in. Jarvis Lorry emerges in a few strokes as a rather distinctive character. Madame Defarge is bloodless, like Lucie and Charles, but for a different reason: She is a cold, vengeful machine seeking to destroy all before her. She remains one of Dickens' most striking creations.

Of the other two major male characters, there exists some difference of opinion. Edgar Johnson finds that Dr. Manette, "though sharply and penetratingly observed, is but an outline in comparison with, say, Mr. Dorrit [in *Little Dorrit*] who is so subtly and sensitively developed." He finds it "rather evident" that Dickens identified himself most with Sydney Carton, for Dickens, in his own life, searched for love, warmth, and understanding and despaired of ever finding it. Carton, the suffering and heroic soul who feels within himself a deep sense of guilt and remorse and the need for atoning for his sins, attains this love, warmth, and understanding, though he must become a martyr to do it. Kitton, too, states that Dickens had a particular liking for Sydney Carton and he quotes the American writer, Richard Grant White, as having said that "there is not a grander and lovelier figure in literature or history." K. J. Fielding (see Bibliography) feels that Dr. Manette is the character that Dickens felt closest to, both because he was an "imprisoned" figure (as Dickens was imprisoned in his domestic situation) and because, like Dickens, Dr. Manette, when in despair, felt a compulsive need for action, for it was "the character of his mind to be always in singular need of occupation."

SIGNIFICANCE OF SUBJECT MATTER

Some critics have believed that there was a great political significance in Dickens' writing a novel about the French Revolution, as a fully developed work of social protest, elements of which has appeared in earlier novels. But Dickens, though he probably believed in the possibility of an uprising in England, stuck to the main theme of the story and avoided the obvious parallels that he might have used if he had an axe to grind in writing this novel. The significance of the novel as a whole is too great to try to find personal opinions in it, either of Dickens or Carlyle. In any case, as Johnson points out, the conflict between love and hate, between revolution and sacrifice, in the end gives Carton's martyrdom a personal grandeur that takes away from the social criticism of the story, and, despite its power, half destroys its revolutionary significance.

THE NOVEL'S LACK OF COMEDY

A criticism frequently made against *A Tale of Two Cities* is that it lacks humor. No one can deny the truth of the statement but it does not seem to be a legitimate complaint. True, humor is an obvious component of most of Dickens' other novels, and many of Dickens' greatest creations are comic characters. It does not necessarily follow, however, that therefore there should be some great comic characters in *A Tale of Two Cities*. Strong humor would be out of place in this story. And, though Jerry Cruncher and Miss Pross do add a leavening of humor to the serious tone of the book, no one can legitimately state that Dickens intended them to be funnier than they turned out to be but failed in his intentions. Ironically, those people who have not read much Dickens enjoy *A Tale of Two Cities* most, while ardent Dickens advocates are disappointed with it as compared to his other works, largely because of the missing element of humor. This lack of humor was particularly objected to by George Gissing (see Bibliography), a noted Dickens authority. He writes, "*A Tale of Two Cities* is not characteristic of Dickens in anything but theme (the attack on social tyranny). With humour lacking we feel the restraint throughout." In the end, the book "leaves no strong impression on the mind; even the figure of Carton grows dim against a dimmer background."

POINTS OF STYLE

Dickens is a story-teller, first and foremost. He was always so in his novels and is particularly so in *A Tale of Two Cities*. Here the story is the thing, and his style is subordinated to it. He is often verbose and redundant, but his style has vigor, clearness, soundness of construction. Dickens was a master of the English language; his prose is finished, well-chosen, and idiomatic. His landscape drawing is very fine: The description of the village and the chateau is very slight but singularly vivid and complete. He is a master of imagery: Stone faces, blood-red fountain, crimson dawn, blue flies searching for carrion, a golden thread, spectre-white dust covering the figure under the Marquis' coach—all these help to fuse and concentrate the novel's themes and incidents.

Dickens was a master of description. To quote Gissing, "Dickens had easy graphic power, wonderfully minute observation. His literary method is that of all the great novelists. To set before his reader the image so vivid in his own mind, he simply describes and reports. We have, in general, a very precise and complete picture of externals—the face, the gesture, the habit. In this Dickens excels; he proves to us by sheer force of visible detail, how actual was the mental form from which he drew. We learn the tone of voice, the trick of utterance; he declared that every word spoken by his characters was audible to him. Then does the man reveal himself in colloquy; sometimes once for all, sometimes by degree, in chapter after chapter—though this is seldom the case. We know these people because we see and hear them."

"SENTIMENTALITY" IN WRITING

Two other frequent criticisms of the book that we should touch on here are: (1) the sometimes unbearable sentimentality, and (2) the over-frequent use of coincidence in the working out of the plot.

The first is a complaint often heard, with much justice. Both Edgar Johnson and K. J. Fielding single out the garret scene where Lucie Manette first sees her father after his release from the Bastille. In Fielding's words, "the scene seems derivative and conventional. Though excellent theater, the dialogue too often has many of the pretentious faults of Victorian drama: just when it ought to carry emotional depth and conflict it begins strumming on stock phrases until released by action." And Johnson: "The scene is marred by the literary artifice of Lucie's tearful rhythmic expressions, 'Weep for it, weep for it.'" The criticism is a just one, particularly of this one scene, which probably even the most romantic reader would find hard to swallow. Johnson's statement that Carton's death is, for many readers, "drenched in over-indulged sentiment," is probably an exaggeration. It has quite a different mood from the garret scene and, somehow, words that in other circumstances would seem mawkish, here attain a splendor and nobility, and the closing segment is, as it was meant to be, the most affecting part of the book.

The second criticism (concerning the use of coincidence) is, if one considers it logically, a legitimate one—Defarge, leader of the Revolution and former servant of Dr. Manette; Madame Defarge, the younger sister of the doomed pair killed by the Marquis Saint Evrémonde and wife of Ernest Defarge; Darnay's return to Paris, and danger, from a safe haven in London; Defarge's discovery of Dr. Manette's diary intact when a similarly unearthed paper had crumbled to dust; Barsad, Miss Pross' long-lost brother, turning up in Paris; and, finally, Carton's looking so much like Darnay that a switch is made without being detected—certainly all of them are a lot to swallow in one gulp. But somehow they get by in the context of the story, and Dickens' skill sees to it that we don't pause as we come to each one and consider its legitimacy before we continue reading. Instead, they all appear in their proper places and they seem quite right and natural when they do appear.

SUMMARY

A Tale of Two Cities is, in Stephan Leacock's words, "a great book despite its imperfections." It has been read and enjoyed by millions of people, and it will doubtless continue to be one of Dickens' most popular novels for many years to come. For, though critics may point out any number of technical imperfections in the book, the power of the narrative is such that even the most laconic reader cannot fail to be caught up in it.

ESSAY QUESTIONS AND ANSWERS

Question
To what extent does Dickens sympathize with the revolutionaries?

Answer
Dickens sympathized greatly with the common people's suffering under the old regime. However, he is as horrified as Mr. Lorry at the lengths to which their violence goes once it is unleashed.

Dickens' first portrait of the common people is in a poor neighborhood in Paris, at a moment when a cask of wine has burst open. As he details the delight and glee with which the Parisians drink up every drop of the wine, and contrasts this moment to their usual hopeless depression, it is clear that he is outraged at their suffering and starvation. His portrait of the condition to which Dr. Manette is reduced after eighteen years of solitary confinement is distressing. On the Marquis' estate, far outside Paris, conditions are even worse—Dickens' sympathy is entirely with these ragged peasants. The haughtiness and callousness of the Marquis contribute a good deal to the reader's anger at the aristocracy and eagerness to see the old regime go down.

However, Dickens paints the excesses of the revolutionary zeal as a nightmare in which many good and innocent people are caught. The guillotine is personified throughout the novel as La Guillotine, a monster with her jaws always open for more food. The only characters the reader meets personally who die at the guillotine are Darnay (the intended victim), who is sentenced to death for the sins of his fathers, and a seamstress, who seems entirely innocent of any wrongdoing.

The death of old Foulon on Bastille Day and the attitude of Madame Defarge toward the Manette family exemplify Dickens' attitude. His vivid description of Foulon's death at the hands of a bloodthirsty crowd who stuffed grass in his mouth horrifies the reader, no matter how much one may feel that Foulon, who once told the starving peasants to eat grass if they were hungry, deserves to be punished. Madame Defarge's intent to destroy Lucie, little Lucie, and Dr. Manette is too misdirected for Dickens or the reader to sympathize with her, despite the fact that her anger over the murder of her family is entirely justified. Dickens entirely supports and even cheers the stabbing of the Marquis, one feels, but not the extermination of innocent members of the Marquis' family.

Question
What is Dickens' greatest achievement in this novel?

Answer
Dickens has plotted his novel with great care; every scene, every incident, and every character, however minor, is essential to its resolution. It is an exciting, fast-paced story with a great deal of action. Dickens has created several memorable personalities, particularly Carton and the formidable Madame Defarge. However, his finest work in this novel relates to the atmosphere he creates of darkness, danger, secrecy, and violence.

Many of the novel's most crucial scenes in the novel take place at night or in dark rooms: the Dover mail journey; the garret in which Defarge has housed the recently released Manette; Stryver's chambers; the tavern where Darnay and Carton confront one another after the trial; Darnay's cell; the cemetery in which Jerry and his associates disinter Cly's coffin; the bedroom in Soho where Manette has his first relapse; Lorry's Paris office. In the darkness, characters cannot clearly see one another, nor what may lie in the shadows. Lorry cannot even be certain that Darnay was not one of the two men beside whom he sat in a coach journey of several hours.

Most of the characters are in danger of one sort or another

throughout the novel. All the French revolutionaries are in danger from the old regime, as the slaughter of Gaspard's child makes clear. By the same token, all the aristocrats are in danger once the common people have given way to their fury. Manette is constantly in danger of relapsing into his bewildered mental wanderings, particularly once he admits Darnay into his circle. Barsad lives an extremely precarious life of spying and lying. Jerry Cruncher's illegal grave-robbing endangers him and his family.

Dickens spins out the secrets of his plot until nearly the end of the novel. The reader is kept in suspense about the cause of Manette's imprisonment and the identity of his accusers until nearly the end of Book Three. Jerry's grave-robbing is alluded to in Chapter 2 of Book One, but not revealed until midway through Book Two. Dickens establishes a mysterious link between Darnay and Dr. Manette, but he does not explain it until near the novel's conclusion. Madame Defarge's personal stake in the extermination of the Evrémondes is not even hinted at until after Darnay's conviction. Characters also keep secrets from one another. Darnay tells no one his true name except Dr. Manette. Carton tells only Lucie of his love for her, and he tells no one of his scheme to save Darnay's life. Jerry tells no one of his grave-robbing until he is caught in his story of Cly in Book Three.

A Tale of Two Cities is a novel of violence, from Jerry's abuse of his long-suffering wife to the slaughter of the prisoners in the jails of Paris. All of the crowd scenes are violent. Barsad, Cly's sole "mourner," nearly loses his life in Cly's funeral procession. The crowds at all three of Darnay's trials are eager for a Guilty verdict and a gory execution—even in the second trial, when Darnay is acquitted, the crowd's enthusiasm and support is described in terms of violence. Even the small moments are violent, such as Lorry's destruction of the shoemaking bench and the Dover mail driver's reaction as Jerry rides up to intercept the coach.

Question

How does *A Tale of Two Cities* differ from Dickens' novels?

Answer

A Tale of Two Cities stands out among Dickens' novels for several reasons: its length, the size of its cast of characters, its mood, its time period, and its focus.

A Tale of Two Cities is considerably shorter than most of Dickens' novels. *David Copperfield, Bleak House, Little Dorrit, Our Mutual Friend, Nicholas Nickleby, The Old Curiosity Shop*—all these novels are substantially longer than *A Tale of Two Cities*. Dickens did write other short novels, such as *Hard Times* and *A Christmas Carol*, but for the most part his novels are extremely lengthy. *A Tale of Two Cities* is atypically brief.

The number of characters in the novel is unusually small. Dickens is famous for his endless parades of minor characters, usually well-drawn, distinct eccentrics like Jerry Cruncher, Stryver, or Miss Pross. *The Old Curiosity Shop* and *The Pickwick Papers* are good examples of crowded novels.

A Tale of Two Cities, on the other hand, has barely a dozen characters. In most of Dickens' novels, characters are added to maintain the reader's interest and to make scenes and locations more colorful and picturesque. In *A Tale of Two Cities*, Dickens includes only characters who affect the plot in one way or another. This economy of characters helps keep the novel far more concise than most of his other novels. The novel has two cities, but only one plot; usually, Dickens alternated installments of his novels between two plots. *The Old Curiosity Shop* reports by turns on Dick Swiveller and Little Nell; half of *Bleak House* is narrated by Esther, concentrating on her own story line, and half by Dickens. When *Nicholas Nickleby* was dramatized for the stage during the 1980s, it ran nearly eight hours. *A Tale of Two Cities* has been filmed several times, and its story is always played out in less than three hours.

Although Dickens was quite capable of creating somber and depressing scenes and stories, none of his other novels is primarily a tale of violence. This is related to the fact that *A Tale of Two Cities* is Dicken's only historical novel: All the others were set in his own time, and are tales of private life. *A Tale of Two Cities* is, of course, the story of the Manettes, the Saint Evrémondes, and Defarges, but these characters are caught up in a vast public event, the Revolution, and the novel is as much a story of the historical event as it is of the characters.

Question

Most of Dickens' works appeared in serial form initially. Do you feel that the structure of *A Tale of Two Cities* was determined by this factor?

Answer

Undoubtedly, *A Tale of Two Cities* was constructed to conform to the requirements of serialization, as it probably could be shown Dickens' other works were. When one is writing a segment of a story for readers, there are several elements that must be present—there must be a certain amount of pathos, a certain amount of humor, a dash of this, a pinch of that, so that the segment will stand as a unity; and the story must be developed in such a way that the reader will want to read the next installment. These narrative strategies are frequently used by Dickens in *A Tale of Two Cities*, though in a much more subtle way. A chapter is closed with some puzzling statement or bit of information that promises to be cleared up in the next installment: for example, Jerry Cruncher's remark, "You'd be in a blazing bad way if recalling to life was to come into fashion, Jerry!" One wonders what significance this has. Or, the words "To be buried alive for eighteen years!" which close Chapter Three. What does it mean? Or, much later, at Darnay's second hearing: "The paper was read, as follows." And there the chapter ends. Who would not be waiting at the magazine stand the next week when the new issue came out, to learn the contents of Dr. Manette's diary?

Question
London and Paris are prominent in the title of the novel. How do the cities function as characters in the story?

Answer
Dickens paints detailed portraits of two widely different cities through description and through the use of crowd scenes such as Cly's funeral parade in London and the storming of the Bastille in Paris.

The reader's first sight of Paris is the gloomy neighborhood of Saint Antoine. Dickens gives a detailed description of the ragged inhabitants, the roughly paved streets, the smells, the grime, and the shabby condition of the streets and houses. This Paris is very different from the "City of Lights" of which one normally thinks. Later scenes of the city center around the Bastille and the guillotine, and they are violent, loud, chaotic, and frightening.

London is portrayed as a refuge, but only to an extent. It can be as dangerous as Paris. Dickens contrasts the quiet of Soho Square with the bustle of Fleet Street and the Strand, and with the mob at the Old Bailey.

The London mobs are as violent as the Paris ones. Dickens gives the reader two major sequences in which the Londoners, as a mob, play a large part: the Old Bailey trial and Cly's funeral procession. The first crowd eagerly anticipates a conviction and a particuarly gruesome execution: The chapter in which Darnay is acquitted is titled "A Disappointment" and ends with the crowd seeking other prey. Cly's funeral shows the same crowd after a successful hunt, turning a funeral into a carnival.

BIBLIOGRAPHY

In addition to the books listed below, there are five periodicals devoted exclusively to articles on the life and work of Dickens. These are *The Dickensian*, the *Dickens Quarterly*, *Dickens Studies*, the *Dickens Studies Newsletter*, and the *Dickens Studies Annual.*

Ackroyd, Peter. *Dickens* (1990).

Allen, Michael. *Charles Dickens' Childhood* (1988).

Barnard, R. *Theme and Imagery in the Novels of Dickens* (1974).

Bentley, Nicholas, *et al. The Dickens Index* (1988).

Burke, Edmund. *Reflections on the Revolution in France* (1790).

Carlyle, Thomas. *The French Revolution* (1837).

Chancellor, E. Beresford. *Dickens and His Times* (1937).

Chesterton, G. K. *Appreciations and Criticism of the Works of Charles Dickens* (1911).

———. *Charles Dickens: A Critical Study* (1906).

Christian, Mildred G. "Carlyle's Influence Upon the Social Theory of Dickens," *Trollopian* (March 1947).

Christie, O. F. *Dickens and His Age* (1939).

Cockshut, A. O. J. *The Imagination of Charles Dickens* (1961).

Cruikshank, Robert J. *Charles Dickens and Early Victorian England* (1949).

Fielding, K. J. *Charles Dickens: A Critical Introduction* (1958).

Ford, George H. *Dickens and His Readers* (1955).

———, and Lauriat Lane, Jr., eds. *The Dickens Critics*, (1961).

Gissing, George R. *Critical Studies of the Works of Charles Dickens* (1924).

Glancy, Ruth F. A Tale of Two Cities: *An Annotated Bibliography* (1993).

———. A Tale of Two Cities: *Dickens' Revolutionary Novel* (1991).

Gregory, Allene. *The French Revolution and the English Novel* (1915).

Gross, John, and Gabriel Pearson, eds. *Dickens and the Twentieth Century* (1962).

Hardy, Barbara. *Dickens: The Later Novels* (1968).

Jarmuth, Sylvia. *Dickens' Use of Women in His Novels* (1967).

Johnson, Edgar. *Charles Dickens: An Introduction to His Novels* (1977).

Kaplan, Fred. *Dickens: A Biography* (1988).

Lucas, John. *The Melancholy Man: A Study of Dickens' Novels* (1970).

Matz, Bertram W. *The Great Victorian Writers: Dickens the Novelist, Carlyle the Philosopher* (1905).

Maurois, Andre. *Dickens* (1935).

Miller, Joseph H. *Charles Dickens: The World of His Novels* (1959).

Orwell, George. *Dickens, Dali and Others* (1946).

Pearson, Hesketh. *Dickens: His Character, Comedy and Career* (1949).

Pope-Hennessey, Una. *Charles Dickens* (1946).

Readings on *A Tale of Two Cities* (1997).

Sanders, Andrew. *Charles Dickens, Resurrectionist* (1982).

———. *The Companion to* A Tale of Two Cities (1988).

Stone, Harry, ed. *Dickens' Working Notes for His Novels* (1987).

Sucksmith, Harvey. *The Narrative Art of Charles Dickens* (1970).

Symons, Julian. *Charles Dickens* (1951).

Zambrano, A. L. *Dickens and Film* (1977).

NOTES

NOTES

NOTES

NOTES

NOTES

NOTES

NOTES

NOTES